THE

Forgotten Ones

GREG HANNLEY

with CALEB ALEXANDER

Cover design by Davida Baldwin/Oddball Design
Interior design by Jessica Tilles/TWA Solutions
Editing by Alana Boutin

ISBN: 978-0-9890349-3-7

To my loving wife, Andrea, my son, Vincent, and my daughter, Hannah.

To my mom and dad, and to my sisters, Heather and Maureen.

To everyone who has ever struggled from the terrible disease of addiction, as well as to those who loved them through their long nightmare.

THE
Forgotten Ones

CHAPTER 1

P eople forget things. Dads forget to take out the trash. Moms forget their keys. We forget cell phones on tables at restaurants. I've even forgotten change for the parking meter once or twice in my life. My parents forgot me and left me behind on a military base at the age of six when our family moved to Tucson. I'll let that sink in for a moment. The seventh of eight kids, my parents simply forgot me. Once the gravity of what happened to me set in, I knew exactly how I was going to spend the rest of my life; I was going to spend it trying to never be forgotten again.

My story began in 1960. My actual journey began six years later, at the tender age of six. I arrived home from school to find my family gone. Not missing, not out shopping—but gone. My father was retiring from the air force after twenty years. He had just wrapped up his last duty station, serving as base commander for Barksdale Air Force Base in Shreveport, Louisiana. My family had purchased a home in Tucson, with the intention of one day returning after my dad's retirement. I hadn't known it at the time, but Dad's retirement had come, and just like that, our service to the nation was over. Back then, kids weren't included in the decisions. There were no discussions, no family meetings, no touchy-feely feel-good exercises about letting kids feel like they were involved in the decisions. Dad said it was time to go, so we went. Dad got orders, and then gave us ours. Simple.

"You can't stay here," the woman said, peering through the screen door.

I peered up from my seat on the front steps of what had been my home when I left for school that morning.

"You have to go," she said, opening the door and stepping outside.

I was six years old. She was the new base commander's wife. It wasn't that she didn't care, it was that the base was fenced in and considered safe for all children no matter their age. We were in a military community, and it was a different time, a different age, a different era, if you will. It was before the tragedy of Adam Walsh. There still existed an innocence within the country about the safety of children.

I don't remember being scared, or nervous, or even that deeply concerned about my circumstances. Even at age six, I was independent. Back then, kids weren't coddled. Military kids, even less so. Being the seventh of eight kids brought out one's independence. The older siblings got to do the bossing around, the youngest was the baby, while those of us trapped in the middle were forced to survive. It was the middlings like me who clawed and scrapped and barreled our way through life, vying for attention, trying not to get lost in the shuffle, trying not to get left behind. That had long been a recurring theme in my life. That desire for attention. That desire to not be passed over, that desire to let the world know that I was here. That desire to not get left behind.

"Run along now," she said, shooing me away.

I rose from the steps, headed down the walkway, thinking about what would come next. It wasn't a panic, just a methodical mental processing of my circumstances. I knew that if I couldn't stay at my old home, I would have to find someplace else. And I knew just where that someplace else would be. It was the other place where I felt comfortable.

I used to play Chinese Checkers at General Wade's house. General Wade was one of those outsized characters who loomed larger than life. He was one of the generals assigned to the Strategic Air Command's 2nd Air Force which was headquartered on the base. The thing I remember most about the general was his Chinese Checker set that he allowed me to play with from time to time. It was one of those old-school ones, made out of the round tin can with the colorful star painted on top. Colorful marbles functioned as the chess pieces. Red, yellow, white, green, blue, and black marbles. My favorite color was blue. I always used the blue ones.

I remember marching up to Mrs. Wade, the general's wife, and asking her if I could live with them. I explained to her what had happened, and like all adults, she thought that I was embellishing my situation with childlike melodrama. But she was a general's wife; there was no problem too large that she couldn't resolve with a phone call. And so she did.

The MPs pulled up to her door and collected me and my school books, and I found myself riding in a police car. It was the first time I had ever been inside of one, but little did I know at the time that it certainly wouldn't be the last.

The MPs kindly dropped me off at temporary housing, where I found my family. It was only when I showed up that they even realized my absence. I, the seventh of eight children, had simply gotten lost in the chaos of the move. Retirement, relocation, good-byes to close friends, the to-do list for tying up our life in Louisiana and starting a new one in Tucson had simply overwhelmed my parents. Again, some dads forget to take out the trash, some moms forget their car keys, some forget slightly more important things.

We never talked about the forgetting. We never talked about a lot of things. And at six years old, I never thought about the psychological aspects of being forgotten during a family move across the country. I didn't even know until much later in my life how much it affected me. All I knew was that I was always searching my pockets, always checking things two, three, even four times. All I knew was that I had a fear of forgetting things. I had a fear of being forgotten. I had a fear of being caught without, or being left in the storm without shelter, without an umbrella, without a plan. Without a word spoken between us about the previous day's events, my family picked up and left for Tucson the next morning.

Tucson...

We arrived in Tucson and immediately jumped into the middle of things. School was in session, and since Dad was retired it was his duty to drop me off. I remember that first day of school like it was yesterday, but only because it affected me almost as deeply as getting left behind on the base. I remember it so well because only four days after our move from Louisiana to Tucson, I got lost.

My Dad didn't have any change to give me for lunch money, so he told me to just walk home for lunch. It was apparent that Dad had forgotten that we weren't living on base anymore, and so there was no safe fence to hem me in and keep me from straying too far. Me, I thought it was a neat idea, until I remembered that I didn't know my way home.

I left school and headed in the direction in which I thought home was. It didn't take me long to realize that I was completely lost. I come across a school eventually, and I'm overcome with relief, until I notice that the tether balls out front are a different color, and I realize that it's not my school that I've come across. I see the mountains in the distance, and I know that I'm lost, so the first thought that comes to my mind, is that I'm going to have to go and live in the mountains. At that age, that's what I thought lost kids did, they went and lived in the mountains. I decided to give it a little longer before my self-banishment, so I keep walking. Eventually, I came across another school, but I knew instantly that this was not my school; this school had a steeple and a church attached to it. I turn in the direction of the mountains and head down a street where I see this red jeep that looked familiar. It was a jeep that I had seen parked across the street from my house. I knew that this was not my street, however, but I knew that jeep.

I walked to the door of the house where the jeep was parked and knocked on the door. It was answered by a woman with a kind face, who was about the age of my mother.

"Ma'am, do you know me?" I asked.

"No."

Dejected, I turned and began to walk away.

"Come here, young man," she said gently. I turned back to her. "What's the matter?"

"I'm lost," I told her. I pointed at the 4X4. "That jeep was at the house across the street."

"That's my son's jeep," she said with a smile. "Hold on."

The woman turned and called her son downstairs. He bounds down the stairs with all the agility of youth, and peers down at me.

"Do you know this young man?" she asked.

"No," he answered, shaking his head.

"He saw your jeep across the street from his house."

"Oh!" the son exclaimed, letting out a knowing smile. "There's a new family that moved across the street from the Cohen's."

His mother smiled, and the two of them loaded me into her son's jeep. He drove me toward my house, where we ran into my sisters Heather and Patsy at the corner. They were in my Dad's Cadillac. I get inside of the car with my sisters, who don't show an ounce of concern. They drive me back to my school, where I've missed lunch. Patsy tells me to wait at the school until my sister Heather gets there to walk me home. Needless to say, the entire way home, my sister Heather and her friend Sally Cohen ran and hid from me, causing me to get lost about five more times on the way home. My first day of school in Tucson, was one of the most traumatic experiences of my life.

Tucson itself, in the seventies, was like any other American city at the time. It was pure Americana, but with a Southwest flavor to it. We had fantastic schools, wonderful communities, neighborhood barbecues, picnics, swim meets, awe-inspiring Fourth of July celebrations, well-lit Nativity scenes in everyone's yards during Christmas. The weather in Tucson even seemed as though it had been preprogrammed to a cookie-cutter setting; it stayed warm, and everyone in the community took advantage of it. We lived our lives outdoors. In our desert utopia, dads lived on the golf courses, while the mothers and the children lived at their local parks. For us, that park was Highland Vista Park.

Highland Vista Park and the park pool was where everyone gathered and swam and played and socialized. We had our own swim team, a dive team, a rec center with a snack bar, which is where my sister worked, as well as family night every Sunday evening. Everyone in the community was a member of Highland Vista community park.

What I remember most about my desert Americana is the freedom that it brought me. I was no longer confined within the interior perimeters of a military base, and I was free to explore, which I did in spades. I lived on my bicycle.

My mother spent her time transporting eight kids around to soccer games, softball games, football games, etc. . . ., going to PTA meetings and selling real estate, while Dad spent his time drinking heavily and beating the hell out of a little white ball, which, in turn, left us kids to our own devices. My father, I think, retired way too early, and was left with more time than he knew what to do with. At least until he took a job selling insurance. So he spent much of his time on the golf course and at the country club, reliving the glory days of his military career through his stories to others. Although we were all fiercely independent, leaving eight kids to their own devices would have disastrous consequences for all of us. We were all left to find things to do to occupy our time, and while some of us found positive ways, others didn't. My sister Heather was introduced to heroin almost immediately upon our arrival.

Tucson was a city that was wide open. It still had that little bit of that Arizona Old West mentality to it. There was desert just outside of the city. Heck, there was desert *inside* of the city. In between my home and the high school I would eventually attend, there was desert. And the desert played a big part in the life of the city. If you weren't a kid at one of the parks playing or swimming, you were a teenager hanging out in the desert with your buddies getting high or making out. That was the non-Americana life in Tucson. It was the life that parents of teens didn't talk about at the barbecues or at family night on Sundays. Back then, families kept secrets, and upholding your family's name was of paramount importance. Regardless of the fact that every other family was dealing with the same issues, some things just weren't talked about. In Tucson, that something was drugs.

I spent my early years in my new city staying away from home. I was at everyone else's home. I don't know if it came from my fear of being left alone and needing a backup home, just in case, or if was just that I liked everyone else's home better than my own. I do know that I had developed a fear of not having money, and that I was always, even at the age of eight, trying to find ways to keep money in my pockets. Being a bike rider, I thought that decorating my bike with those old STP stickers that they gave away at gas stations was way cool, and I learned that everyone else thought so as well. The thing is, most of the kids my age didn't have the freedom that I had and couldn't leave their neighborhood to go and get any. I also learned that kids were willing to pay for these stickers. I spent a lot of time on my bicycle riding around town collecting STP stickers and selling them to other kids. It was my first hustle.

Sell, sell, sell. While most people would recognize it as the mantra on Wall Street, it was also my mantra. The mantra of an eight-year-old kid in 1970s Tucson. I was always trying to sell something. I was desperate to keep money in my pockets, just in case. I climbed trees, cut mistletoe, bagged it, and sold it during the Christmas season. At the age of nine, I started selling American Seeds to supplement my income from selling STP stickers. By the time I was twelve, I was selling Coca-Cola, candy, peanuts, and popcorn at the ballpark. It was all fantastic money for a ten-year-old, and it fueled my desire to make more. At the age of twelve, I sold my first newspaper, and little did I know it at the time, but selling print media would have a profound effect on my life.

I developed my own paper route around the age of twelve. I didn't wait for someone to give me a paper route, nor did I wait for something so mundane as people to actually subscribe to the newspaper. That was not my style. I would throw *Grit* newspapers to people's home who I knew weren't subscribers, and, of course, they would keep the newspapers. And so, I would kindly go to their door during collection time with my little flip pad and collect for the newspapers I had thrown them. It taught me a couple of lessons that I would carry with me forever. One, people didn't know what they wanted until you showed them, and two, where there is no demand, you create it. I used these lessons, and at the age of twelve, I kept my pockets full of just-in-case money. Life was good . . . except at home. At the tender age of fourteen, my sister became a heroin addict.

Heroin in the seventies was not as widespread as it is now. People didn't know a lot about it, and it didn't have the stigma that it now has, but it was just as addictive and just as destructive. My sister started off with pot, like most people do, and then gradually progressed to stronger and stronger drugs. Just like I was always seeking that extra dollar to provide me a sense of security, she was seeking that stronger and stronger narcotic to provide her with a sense of well-being. We both had our insecurities; mine was money, hers was drugs. Who's to say which was more destructive and addictive?

My sister's pot-smoking buddies became her heroin-addicted buddies over time. They lounged around the community park, pretty much in a catatonic state, dazed out of their minds and seemingly multiplying like bunnies. They were few in number at first, but over time, slowly grew in number until we were practically tripping over them in the park. I caught them shooting up so many times that eventually that too became a racket for me. They would pay me to keep my silence.

Parents, you're probably wondering, where in the heck were my parents? They were being typical '70s parents. Mom had eight kids to raise, so there was soccer practice, softball practice, two kids in college, and a rocketing career in residential real estate. Dad had his golf clubs. And scotch. Dad had his scotch. The two of them together, scotch and golf, often made for an awkward combination. Even embarrassing in some instances.

"C'mon," Dad told me. "Where are we going?" I asked.

I had better things to do. I had my own life and my own things going on. I dreaded having to participate in a father-son moment. My dad remained silent. Back then, kids weren't given explanations; we simply did what we were told. I climbed into my dad's Cadillac, and we took off, headed to some unknown destination.

We arrived at the golf course, and I thought that it was another case of Dad wanting to give me more golf lessons. There were way more exciting things that I could be doing than carrying Dad's golf bag and keeping silent, while he "taught" me how to play golf.

"Let's go," Dad said, climbing out of his Caddy. He went to the back of the car, opened the trunk, and pulled out a long rope that was wound into a tight circle. He definitely had my curiosity.

I followed my father through the parking lot and onto the course, where we crossed over the greens and made our way to a lake on the course.

"Take off your clothes," Dad commanded.

"Huh?"

"Hurry up!" he said, growing impatient. "Take off your clothes so they won't get wet!"

I peered around the golf course to see if anyone was watching. I wasn't exactly built like Mr. Atlas or Mr. America at that age, and like any twelve-year-old, I was quite modest. I hesitated, until I saw that my father was serious. Then I began to strip my clothes off.

Dad stopped me once I got to my boxers. The rest of my clothes I had piled up on top of my shoes. Dad then tied the rope around my waist, securing it tightly.

"I want you to fish around in there," he said, pointing toward the lake. "I lost my nine iron. And get me some balls out of there if you find some. Should be plenty in there."

I couldn't believe that he was serious—but he was. The smell of cigars and alcohol on his breath had me doubting the entire situation for a brief moment, and then he urged me along.

I climbed into the murky waters of the lake and swam to the middle with the rope tied around my waist and began to dive and search for my dad's golf club.

"You find it?" he shouted when I came up for air.

I wiped the murky water from my face and shook my head. "Well, hurry up!" he shouted. "It's in there somewhere!"

I went back under the water, and I searched until my lungs almost burst. I was determined not to surface without finding Dad's golf club. And apparently, he was just as determined. I felt not a single tug on the rope while I was beneath the surface of the water. I rose from the murky depths of the water holding Dad's nine iron in my hand, like I had just retrieved the sword Excalibur.

I made my way to the banks of the lake and handed my father his beloved golf club. I expected a "great job," perhaps an "are you okay?" or maybe even a "thanks." Instead, I got . . .

"Hey, did you find any balls while you were down there?" he asked.

Don't get me wrong about my father. I had a good dad. He was a great father, an outstanding husband, and phenomenal leader. The people under his command loved him, and that included his family. It was a different time, a different era. Men weren't touchy-feely back in those days, especially the colonel.

During that year, my sister and her buddies continued to binge out all over the house, while I spent my time falling in love with Kelley Hannah, a nice Mormon girl who went to my school. I thought Kelley was sent from heaven. She had long brown hair, beautiful brown eyes, and a smile that would melt an iceberg. I thought that I would marry her someday. She was the first girl I ever kissed. I spent many nights calling her house, listening to her voice as she answered the telephone—and then hanging up in panic-stricken fear. I was always awkward and super shy when it came to the opposite sex. My tongue became tied, my words became jumbled, and my brain cells disintegrated within milliseconds of engaging in a conversation with a pretty girl. It was for these reasons that I never got the girl, and why all of the girls I had crushes on ended up on the arms of one of my friends.

As time went on, the money I received as bribes apparently became too much for my sister and her junkie friends, as it began to cut into their heroin money. So, my sister did the one other thing that she could do to keep me from telling; she made me a party to the crime. My sister introduced me to pot at the age of twelve. After that, pot and I became as inseparable as two star-crossed lovers. By the time my thirteenth birthday rolled around, I was officially a pothead.

My early teens were spent hanging out at the Ricos' house, smoking pot, and doing whatever other drugs my sister saw fit to introduce me to in order to keep me quiet. I played baseball, but I wasn't a future MLB Hall of Famer by any stretch of the imagination. I played football, but would never be an NFL Pro Bowler. I was in the Cub Scouts, and that was a part of my life for a while.

Of all the activities that I participated in, the two that I found myself most adept at were golf and tennis. I guess I *had* paid attention to Dad's instructions, after all. And as for tennis, beating the shit out of little balls seemed to just run in my family. Golf ball, tennis balls, heroin balls . . . I became so good at tennis, that I eventually would make the varsity team in high school, during my freshman year.

My sister's deep dive into addiction was eventually discovered by my parents. It devastated them. Like all parents, they wondered where they went wrong and blamed themselves for everything that happened. And like all families dealing with these types of things during the '70s, we kept our struggles quiet. We kept them quiet until they couldn't be kept quiet any more. My sister's boyfriend, Mike Marconi, took his own life by overdosing on heroin.

Of my sister's binge buddies, I liked Mike the most. He was someone I could talk to. He paid attention to me, and he became like an older brother to me. It felt as if my heart had been ripped from my body when Mike killed himself. And the tragedy of it all was that it didn't have to happen. It was the pressure of youth and youthful mistakes that took him.

Mike's mother worked in a drugstore, and it was Mike who gave his friends the information they needed to pull off the robbery of the store in order to obtain the cash they needed to fuel their drug binge. Heroin addict or not, Mike had a conscience, and his part in the robbery ate him up on the inside. What many people forget is that people who are addicts are still people. Mike was a good person. He feared that his mother was going to find out that it was *his* friends that robbed her drugstore. It was too much for a seventeen-year-old to deal with. He placed a needle in his vein and ended all of his worries.

The fear that struck my parents after Mike's death was palpable. They saw their daughter lying in that casket but for the grace of God. It was too much for my father. He did the only thing that he knew how to do. After everything else had failed, he went back to being the warrior that he was. I watched my father pull out his gun and head out the door.

Dad went to Bernie Alvarado's house, my sister's and Mike's supplier, stuck his gun in Bernie's mouth, and told him that if he ever came around my sister again, he would blow his head off. Needless to say, Bernie stayed away. My parents got my sister on methadone, and eventually got her off heroin.

Everyone was focused on my sister, which left me to glide under the radar. I continued to smoke like a broken stove, and eventually, my grades began to reflect my pot smoking. I quickly learned to intercept my report card and manipulate my grades. My buddies and I spent copious amounts of time hanging out in the desert that lay between my neighborhood and the high school, skipping school and getting high.

My high school years came. The fad at that time was tennis. Everyone wanted to play tennis, everyone wanted to be a pro tennis player. It was the time of Arthur Ashe and Johnny Newcombe. Everyone envisioned winning the Grand Slam, or at least the U.S. Open. I too was swept up in the tennis frenzy.

My friend's parents paid happily for their kid's tennis lessons. At $45 a session, there was no way my parents were going to do the same for me. Being that I was never going to get left behind in anything, I devised a way to obtain tennis lessons for myself. I swept the tennis court in exchange for tennis lessons.

I was good at tennis. I was so good that I earned my varsity letter in tennis as a freshman. Tennis even abated my unquenchable thirst for pot Not by much, but by enough that I was able to win some matches. My instructor was even impressed with my abilities. At least he was until I showed up stoned out of my mind one day. After that, he refused to instruct me anymore, and thus, ended my career as a tennis pro.

On the home front, things were progressing well. My older brother Mike had started working for a company called Dial Finance. He had done well enough to eventually land a job at a bank and work his way up to vice president of First National. He promised me a job at the bank once I finished high school. My brother Jim went into the mines and did pretty well for himself. He kept getting promoted, joined the unions, and never being one to half step anything, eventually became a full-fledged, card-carrying communist. It later turned out that communism wasn't for Jim, so he later decided that he wanted to become a priest. Later, my brother Jim got a job managing the airport on the north side of town, and he offered me a job. My job was to basically babysit cars, but involved a multitude of other responsibilities, many of which, a sixteen-year-old kid had no business doing. Let's just say that on my first day, I assigned two planes coming from opposite directions the same runway . . . at the same time. Luckily, the pilots were extremely skilled and blessed that day. I spent the rest of my time at the airport away from the control tower and in the garage where I was supposed to be. But even that job didn't keep me out of trouble. I quickly learned how to hot-wire cars and siphon gas. My ability to do these things ended up getting me into a bit of trouble. At sixteen, I found myself having to attend Catholic Youth Organization, or CYO. The judge gave me a choice: Juvenile or CYO. Naturally, I chose CYO.

CYO wasn't bad. And as time went on, I learned to manipulate that system as well. I got a lot of guys that I knew to join, and eventually, it became popular. We started having dances and taking trips. And since the administrator was legally blind, and I had a driver's license, I was allowed to drive the bus around town on CYO business. Needless to say, that bus quickly became a weed-filled party bus for me and my friends. In fact, we became so used to smoking pot on the bus that it became normal, even with the administrator on board.

My popularity with the priest and the administrator, as well as my experience driving the bus, made me the shoo-in for the sidekick position when it came time for CYO to take a trip to Disneyland. I sat up front next to the bus driver and the bus monitor during the trip. Not being able to turn it off, I brought along a bag of weed. We had a parent along with us as a bus monitor, so I decided that I would wait until we reached the hotel to spark up. My buddy lacked the common sense to do the same. He decided to spark up and smoke on the bus, and was caught by the monitor, who insisted that I had something to do with it. She called my father and blamed the entire situation on me.

I had gotten kind of close to the priests and the staff at CYO during my time there. So much so, that I, like my brother Jim, was even thinking that I may want to enter the priesthood. No, seriously. Well, after the phone call to my father, that idea was pretty much doomed. Upon our arrival back in Tucson, my father and the priest were waiting for us as I pulled the bus into the parking lot. My father pulled me off the bus and beat me in the parking lot. I never went back to church after that.

*Greg Hannley &
Mom*

*Greg Hannley &
Dad*

Colonel Vincent Paul (Doc) Hanley

CHAPTER 2

At the age of seventeen, I saw a Travel USA ad. It promised me plenty of money and an opportunity to travel the country as I made money. It appealed to me. The independence of it . . . the freedom of it . . . the ability to travel and see the country and to make plenty of money while doing it. What about it wouldn't appeal to a seventeen-year-old kid? If only I would have known that it was all bullshit.

I left home after deciding that I was through with school. My older siblings had all done the college thing. My house was basically a way station until you attended the University of Arizona. My older sister, Beth, attended. My older brother, Mike, attended. My younger brother, Rob, would eventually attend. Patsy, and Maureen, attended college in Louisiana. Me . . . I had a different direction in mind. The path I wanted to walk was far from the conventional one. I was still searching for that *extra* something. I was still determined to be independent and to be able to stand on my own two feet when the storm came. I wanted to make sure that I would make it if I ever got left behind.

The Travel USA ad led me to Rick Brock, a character who would loom large in my life and influence me in ways that few others had. Rick was a master salesman, and an even more masterful manipulator. He was the kind of guy who really could sell ice to Eskimos.

The ad in Travel USA promised adventure; it promised the opportunity to make plenty of money, to be independent, to see the country, to make it big. It was all bullshit for the most part. The adventure part was real; the see-the-country part of it was real; the independence part, the freedom part, and the make money part were all bullshit.

I'll make it as simple as I can, without oversimplifying the entire thing. The job was magazine sales. It was for sales crew members who were sent door-to-door to con people into buying magazines. I didn't know it then, but later found out how the entire thing worked. The magazine publishers would send the magazines to clearinghouses, who then sold them to companies who employed sales crews to get rid of them. There were two aspects to the business. One, the cash sales, and the other was the subscription sales. The crew's money came from the door-to-door; the big bosses and owners were paid from this as well. The money that came from subscriptions was just icing on the cake for the big bosses.

We got paid $6 a day during the week, and $10 a day on the weekends. A fortune, right? Like I said before, it was all bullshit. We stayed in seedy motels, we bounced checks, we ate when we could, and we lived on the road like a traveling band of gypsies. The majority of the kids in the business were runaways who just needed a place to stay and something to eat. This provided the sustenance they needed to survive away from home, and not go back to their abusive stepparents, their junky parents, or whatever shithole they ran away from. We were taken advantage of big time by slick groups of con men who used us to get rich.

Being on the road was dangerous. My time with Rick was full of violence, intimidation, and hard times. Rick carried a big, black, semiautomatic pistol, and he was constantly pulling out that gun on everybody. And it wasn't just the pulling of the gun that was intimidating, but the fact that he was willing to use it. I watched many a kid who came up short on their sales quotas get pistol-whipped by Rick. He was not only the crew leader, but also the crew's chief enforcer. Rick inspired fear in each and every one of us, but what's more is that he coupled that fear with motivational speeches. There were speeches about being great salesmen. He would have us write down our long-term goals. He would even have us sing crew songs every morning. It was all very weird and cultlike, and like every other cult that's ever existed, it was impossible to get away from. They put in place physical safeguards from escape in case the mental ones ever broke down.

We weren't allowed to go anywhere alone. If we went to the movies, we had to go together in a group. If you wanted to go to the store, you had to go in a group. And there were always enforcers around; there was always someone watching. For our fifteen-person crew, there was DK, a giant mob-type of guy who just folded his arms and stared menacingly at everyone.

And then there was Bonnie from Dallas, and she was just as dangerous as DK or Rick. If you wanted to leave, you would have to secretly get in touch with your family and have them buy you a Greyhound ticket and have it waiting for you at the bus station. Your escape would have to be done in the dead of night. Rick had made it clear, if you wanted to leave, you were going to be dropped off far out of town, in the middle of nowhere, in the dead of night, on an empty stretch of road, with nothing but a dollar in your pocket. He said it—and he meant it. And it terrified me just as much as the beatings that he gave us for not selling.

My first beatings didn't come right away. They took mercy on me, because they could see how hard I was trying. And when I had pushed their patience to the breaking point, I had people who would step in for me and help me out. I remember this one case in particular.

I was going door-to-door with another Rick. This guy's name was Rick Trammell. This lady's cat ran out, and Rick chased down the cat and caught it. The lady wasn't interested in buying anything from us that day, and I had thrown everything at her. Our usual MO was to tell the customers that we were going to use the money for college, and that the top salesmen would even win a trip to Paris, Rome, or London, and that we're about to win the contest, but we just needed this one last sale to put us over the top. We had lies on top of lies that we were trained to tell people. But despite my throwing everything at her, she just wasn't buying. Rick and I had sold nothing that day. We were both in dire straits. Rick held her cat and told her that he had just found a stray on the street and that he planned on keeping it. He could be convinced to give it to her, if she could find it in her heart to buy a few magazines from us. And he basically sold her back her cat.

The sales belonged to Rick; however, when we got picked up, he told them that they were my sales and that he hadn't made any that day. The fury that was hurled at him was unbelievable. He was threatened, beaten, and then taken away. The most horrific thing in my mind was that after that day, I never saw Rick Trammell again.

Being on the road with Rick's crew was like sticking your arm in a pit full of deadly sea snakes. You never knew when death was going to come, but you knew that it was ever present. It was there at every door you knocked on; it was at the hotel in the evening when Rick was going off in a rage over sales quotas; it was there when you looked into DK's eyes—it was everywhere. I thought that I had found it once on a dark and lonely road in Florida.

We had ventured to Florida. It was Northern Florida, which is more Old South than the Miami and other South Florida areas. Segregation was still in full effect, and somehow, someway, I wound up in an African American community. Well, I did know how I ended up there. The car handler at the time, this mean old bat named Cindy Miley, was pissed off at me, so she dropped me off in the middle of nowhere as payback.

That the community was destitute was clear by the look of the houses. They were ramshackle shotgun houses that looked to be remnants from the previous century. Why Rick thought we could garner magazine sales from a neighborhood whose people were barely surviving was beyond me, but what I did know is that they felt that I didn't belong there just as much as I felt like I didn't belong there. I could hear them asking what this scrawny-looking white boy was doing in their neighborhood.

Word got out that I was just trying to scratch out a living selling magazines, and their looks of suspicion turned to looks of concern. Night began to creep upon us, and streetlights in this community were nonexistent. They, and I, began to fear for my safety.

I came upon a black family who looked to be having a get-together in their front yard. I was invited into the yard, questioned, and then told that it was getting dark and that the streets would be too dangerous for me to walk. They told me that I could stay there with them until my pickup arrived. I was even invited to partake in their meal. It was the first time in my life that I had ever eaten barbecued squirrel.

My trip to Florida, along with the beatings, the threats, the pistol whippings all took a toll on me. I was ready to get away from them; I was ready to go home. I devised an escape plan, and I fled in the middle of the night. All my life, I had a fear of being forgotten, a fear of being left behind, but then, sitting at that Greyhound bus station, I had a fear of being remembered, a fear of being missed, and a fear of being discovered. I made it home to Tucson two days later and slept in my own bed for the first time in more than a year. It was the best sleep I had ever had up until that point. No Rick, no pistol, no worries. I was safe back home with my mother and father under the same roof.

My respite at home was short-lived. I stayed at home for less than a month. It was enough time to recharge, to unwind, to eat and gain a few pounds. In fact, I had just come from dinner with my parents when a car pulled into the driveway and I found Rick sitting on our front porch. Seeing him sitting there pushed away all feelings of relaxation and ease as a tense sense of apprehension overtook my body. I immediately felt as though I was late, I was behind on my sales, and as though I was about to be severely punished. Rick spoke very few words. He simply told me to go and get my stuff. It was time.

The fact that Rick was a master manipulator couldn't fully explain the depth of the hold that he had on me. It was psychologically deeper, more cultlike than manipulative. I simply walked into my home, grabbed my belongings from my room, and left with him. I went back to the beatings, back to the threats, the intimidation, the pistol whippings, the motels, the pressure sales, the hunger, and the danger of life on the road.

My return to Rick's crew aka Union Circulation was pretty much more of the same. The fact that I wasn't a runaway, and that I outlasted all of the others meant that I was able to move up in the ranks. I eventually became a team leader. Being a team leader meant that I had more responsibility, but it also gave me a little more money, and, best of all, took me out of the day-to-day, door-to-door sales routine. I was now responsible for my team, for dropping them off, picking them up, motivating them, teaching them the ins and outs of the business, and just generally being their leader. But being their leader also meant that I would have to keep them in line. Keeping people in line was something that I had never been good at. All my life I kept scary guys around me, just so that I didn't have to be the scary guy that no one messed with. And now, Rick was asking me to be *that* guy.

We had a guy with the crew named Cliff *****. Same rules applied. If you wanted to leave the crew, you would be dropped off in the middle of nowhere, in the middle of the night, with nothing but a dollar in your pocket. Unfortunately for Cliff, and for me, Cliff had decided that he wanted to leave.

"Take him out of town and drop his ass off in the middle of the desert," Rick ordered. "And if you don't, I'll know it. I always have people watching. So, if you lie to me, it'll be your ass getting dropped off in the middle of the desert, and it won't be with a dollar in your pocket; it'll be with a bullet in your head."

I nodded, grabbed the keys, and headed out the door with Cliff trailing just behind. I knew what the rules were, and I knew what Rick would do to me if I disobeyed him. Cliff and I climbed inside of the van and set off into the night.

"You don't have to do this!" Cliff pleaded. "Yes, I do," I told him.

"No, you don't!" Cliff said. "You can just drop me off on the edge of town. I won't tell anybody. I swear to you, I won't!"

"Rick's gonna know," I said nervously.

"He won't," Cliff said, turning and peering over his shoulder. "No one's following us. Please! I just wanna go home!"

"Do you know what Rick will do to me?" I asked.

"Do you know what's going to happen to me in the middle of the desert, in the middle of the night?" Cliff replied. "I won't make it back alive. There are all kinds of animals out there. All kinds of bad people. Drifters, weirdos driving by, mafia guys burying bodies. I won't make it. If the bobcats don't kill me, the cold will."

I banged my fist against the steering wheel and pulled to the side of the road.

"Do you know Rick's gonna kill me?" "Please!"

Tears came to his eyes. I held mine back. I leaned my head back against the seat and exhaled forcefully.

"Rick's going to kill me," I said to myself.

I knew that there would be consequences for disobeying Rick, but I also knew that no matter how hard I tried to fake it, or how hard I tried to seem like I was hard, I was just fooling myself. I wasn't going to drop Cliff off in the desert. I wasn't that guy. I wasn't anywhere close to even being that type of guy.

I pulled the van back onto road.

"You better not tell anyone—ever!" I told him.

"I promise you, I won't!" Cliff said. I could hear the relief in his voice.

"You promise me that you won't call the motel?" I asked. "I swear to you!"

"No matter what?"

"No matter what!" he said, reassuring me.

"And don't ever come back!" I told him. "Rick better not ever hear about this or get wind of this, you hear me? As far as anyone is concerned, you got dropped off in the middle of the freaking desert. You understand me?"

Cliff nodded. "I swear. I swear on my life!"

I dropped Cliff off at the Greyhound bus station that night, and then headed back to the motel after driving around a while to kill some time. I had to make it seem like I had taken him to the middle of nowhere. When I got back to the motel, Rick was waiting.

"Where'd you drop him off at?" Rick asked.

"In the desert," I answered. "Just like you told me to."

"You're lying!" Rick shouted. "Do you think I'm dumb? Do you think I'm an idiot? Am I dressed like a court jester?"

I lifted my palms toward him, trying to give him pause. "Rick, I did. I dropped him off, just like you told me!"

Rick pulled out his pistol and grabbed me by my neck. He held my neck with one hand, while placing the gun to my head with his other hand.

"You're lying!" "Rick, I swear!"

"I can't take it when you lie to me!" he shouted. "Just admit it. Admit that you didn't drop him off out of town like I told you to! Admit it, and I won't kill you tonight! Admit it!"

"All right!" I shouted. "Okay, okay, I didn't."

"Where'd you take him to?"

"To the Greyhound station," I answered nervously.

Rick removed the gun from my head and let go of my neck. "Don't ever lie to me, because I'll know it."

I clasped my neck and rubbed it.

"Since you told me the truth, I won't kill you tonight," he continued. "But I'm still going to have to kill you, because you did try to lie to me. It'll come in the future."

And just like that, it was over. Rick turned and started focusing on something else.

I had never had a gun placed against my head before. And I swear that my life flashed before my eyes. I just knew that I was a goner that night. It was typical Rick. Violence. Manipulation. Motivation. He pulled a gun on me for not dropping someone off in the middle of the desert, and then had me feeling like I *owed* him for not killing me. I knew that I had to get away from him and from this crew before he did kill me. That night was the night that I made my decision to escape and to get away for good. The actual straw that broke the camel's back and triggered my escape came a short period later. He ordered me to beat my girlfriend.

Her name was Laurie. She was beautiful. She had red hair and blue eyes and had a complexion like buttermilk. She was a part of the crew. She came on board before I joined, and she and I had started messing around and became an item. Everyone in the crew knew this, despite that fact that we had tried to keep it a secret. Rick had a saying. He believed that there was no love, only lust and weakness. So, on Saturday nights, after drinking and binging, he would assign who would sleep with whom that night. The rule was, you couldn't sleep with the same girl twice.

"Beat her ass," Rick told me. "What?" I asked.

"That bitch has a fucked-up attitude," Rick said. "I don't like the way she talked to me, so go out there, whip her ass, and put her in check."

"Rick, I can't beat up a girl," I protested.

Again, he pulled out his gun. "You beat her, or I'll kill you, and then she still gets her ass beat anyway. You got it? You want me to do it?"

"No," I said, shaking my head. I knew that if he beat her, it would be brutal.

I headed outside of the motel room and searched the premises until I found her. She was standing on a balcony overlooking the swimming pool, drinking a Coke. She was fuming.

"I hate that asshole!" she said, when she saw me.

I walked up to her, stood next to her, and peered over the balcony toward the pool.

"I know," I told her.

"He's such a fucking prick!" she said, after taking a sip from her soda.

"I know," I agreed. I paused for a few moments, not knowing what to say or even how to say it. "He wants me to beat you."

"Oh really?" she asked.

"He pulled out his gun and said that if I didn't come out here and beat you, he would kill me."

Laurie closed her eyes and exhaled. "We could run," I told her.

"And go where?" she asked. "Do what? With what?"

She was right. We were both flat broke. But still, there was no way I was going to hit her or do anything else to cause her harm.

She turned toward me and extended her arms. "Do what you gotta do."

"Laurie, I'm not going to—"

"Hey!" she said, cutting me off. "It's gonna happen. It's gotta happen regardless."

"I can't," I said, shaking my head.

"He's going to hurt you," she said, caressing my cheek. "Better me than you," I told her.

Laurie took another drink from her Coke, and then bashed herself in the eye with it.

"What the hell are you doing?" I said, trying to grab the can.

Laurie moved back quickly and bashed herself in the face several more times before I could get to her. I grabbed the can, and she screamed.

"You bastard! How dare you hit me! I'm going to fuck you up!"

She had shouted it loud enough for everyone in the complex to hear. And if anyone had peered up onto that balcony, it would appear as though we were tussling. Laurie finished the job by messing up her hair, and then raking her nails across her face. She threw the Coke can across the balcony, leaned in, and kissed me on the cheek, and then ran off. She had the appearance of having been beaten. Her beautiful skin had turned red and purple with bruises.

I stood on the balcony of the motel thinking about what had transpired. I had been ordered to beat a girl that I felt as though I was in love with. I had been man enough not to do it, but not strong enough to resist Rick and protect her. I knew that I had to escape.

Not long after Laurie managed to escape, I met this girl named Rene Pennington. She was gorgeous; beautiful hair, gorgeous eyes, electric smile. She had it all. I was thunderstruck. And then came Rick, and his bullshit rules. Rick said that Roger had to sleep with Rene, and that I couldn't be with her. It struck me hard. I remembered asking myself, what kind of business is this? Who are these people, and where do they come from? This business had to change. All of the characters, the business practices, the filth and griminess of it, all had to change. I vowed that I would be the one to change it.

I loved the business, I loved the job, but hated the way that it was being run. I knew that there had to be a better way. It was on that balcony that I promised myself that if I ever got the chance, I would do things differently. That I would make a difference. I promised that I would make a difference. That would all come later. Right now, I knew that I had to get away, I was desperate to get away from Rick and his demented rules and sadistic crew. My friend Mike and I escaped and fled to Tucson a few days later.

The Motley Crew

CHAPTER 3

⊷

My time in Tucson was short-lived. I was restless. I needed to be out on the road. As bad as that life seemed, it was highly addictive. The threats and beatings were bad, but traveling, seeing the country, and meeting people was almost like a natural high. I saw places that most people never knew existed. When most Americans traveled the country; they saw the tourist areas, not the areas where the motels rented rooms by the hour. They didn't get to walk the neighborhoods, venture into the neighborhood stores, get a feel for the people and their communities. America is its people, and I was getting to see America.

I had always been a military brat. I had traveled the world with my parents. Admittedly, I was young when my father retired, but traveling was in my blood. My traveling around Tucson while other kids stayed safely in the neighborhood had only served to prepare me for the travels that I had experienced selling magazines across the country. I was born to go; it was in my blood. Tucson had become suffocatingly small for me, and so I knew that it was only a matter of time before I found a way to leave home again. Besides, all of the guys that I grew up with were gone. And by gone, I don't necessarily mean in the physical sense.

My buddy Raul, whose house I spent a lot of time at growing up, had become addicted to drugs and had started robbing ATM machines. I saw him while I was in town, and he looked bad, really bad. My good friend Mark Holly had gotten shot in the back by the DEA while trying to do a drug deal. It seemed as if just about everyone I had grown up with was freebasing. One of my buddies told me that taking a hit off of that pipe was like having sex with a gorilla; you're not done until the gorilla says you're done. I had to get out of Tucson before I too became a statistic.

My opportunity came when Mike and I saw another Travel USA ad in the newspaper. The time, we knew exactly what it was and exactly what it meant and exactly what we would be doing. It was an ad for another crew. We didn't hesitate.

The new crew was with a company called Tipco. It was owned by two guys named Mike Furhman and Belo Kellum. Tom Daily was the crew manager. This crew was the complete opposite of Rick's crew. And by that, I meant in good ways and bad ways. Gone were the threats and intimidation, and they actually paid people like they were supposed to, when they were supposed to. And if someone wanted to leave, they would actually take them to the bus station, and really buy them a ticket! Twice a year, they would take the crew on vacation. It was almost too good to be true. Those were the good parts. The bad part? It was a drinking, drug-fueled, orgy-having crew.

Whereas Rick would have killed us if we ever thought of using any kind of drugs, with this crew, it was expected. You were supposed to wake up hungover, in bed with a different girl lying next to you. It was complete and total debauchery.

I stayed with Mike Furhman's crew for a while. And things were great. We sold plenty of magazines, we drank hard, partied harder, and stayed getting into all sorts of things. They were crazy days and crazy times. I remember getting my hands on a UPI press badge and getting my crew into White Sox games, movies, and all kinds of events. Half the time we were buzzed or drunk, and just out doing crazy stuff. The owner of the company would roll up the entire company and take us all to Acapulco, Mexico, every Fourth of July. Acapulco during the summer was ridiculous. It was full of young college girls, rich but lonely married women, and Mexican girls looking for a gringo to take them back to America. Tipco, at this time, was like one big merry-go-round of drugs, music, and partying. I had even managed to get promoted a few times in between the partying. It wasn't until I was up for my next promotion when things turned sour.

"What do you . . . You want me to train him?" I asked Mike.

"The boss wants you to train him to be the permanent car handler," Mike replied.

"That's bullshit!" I protested.

"He's the boss's friend," Mike said flatly. "The boss wants him in that position."

"Bullshit!" I said again, this time storming toward the door. "I'm outta here!"

I was pissed because I was up for that promotion. The permanent car handler was the guy who dropped the kids off, and then checked up on them. It was my next step on my way to being a district manager. And not only were they not giving me the position, but they wanted me to train the guy who they were giving it to. A guy who was just coming on board, a guy who had no magazine experience, and whose only qualification was that he was the owner's friend. It was total bullshit. He had never hustled his ass off in the cold, the rain, the snow, and had doors slammed in his face, or had dogs chase him down the street, or had anyone threaten to get their gun if I didn't get off their property. He had never been beaten, or pistol-whipped, or had guns put to his head, or had to bounce checks or be hungry. I had been through all of those things since I started in the industry. I had *earned* that position, and now they wanted me to train the boss's friend to do the job that I had earned? I was out of there. I went to look for my friend Mike Malone.

Mike and I had joined this crew together. We were both from Tucson, and we had even talked about the possibility of this happening. We had both agreed that we would go back to Tucson and find another crew if I was passed over. We were in this together.

Only, I couldn't find Mike. I searched the area, checked with everyone, and still no Mike. After a few hours, I made my way back to the motel that we were staying in. When I walked into the lounge area, Mike Furhman was in his usual place, seated around a table playing gin with his buddies, and getting drunk on Jack Daniels. He called me over.

"Hey, Greg, let me talk to ya."

I walked to where they were seated. I didn't know what to expect, but I knew it was going to be some bullshit.

"So, I called a buddy of mine," Mike continued. "His name's Doug. He's a good guy. He works for Mecca. Doug has a crew in Colorado right now, and they're not too strong. He needs some good guys. He said that he needs a reliable permanent driver, and so we cut a deal."

"You cut a deal?" I asked, lifting an eyebrow.

"Yeah," Mike said, without peering up from his card game. "He's going to slide me some cash, and I'm going to send you out to Denver to be his permanent driver. It's a win for everybody. You get the promotion, he gets a strong, reliable guy, and I get some cash. Doug's a good guy, Greg. You'll like him. And he doesn't have a lot of good guys on his crew. The opportunity for you to climb up the ladder fast is there. You just go and do what you've done here, and you'll shoot up the ladder in no time."

I couldn't believe what he was telling me. He had just sold me to his best friend's crew.

I was put on a plane for Denver that night.

Doug Hennsley's crew was called the Tigers II. They worked for a company out of Texas called Mecca, which was owned by a guy name Joe Edge. Doug was one of those characters who was larger than life. He had an outsized personality, and everyone loved him. Doug had never met a stranger; he was everyone's best friend. I took to him instantly.

Doug's crew was different from Mike's crew. It felt less like a traveling party, and more like a legit business trying to get off the ground. It was much lower key and had a completely different feel to it. Rick's crew felt like you were living under the watchful eye of the Taliban, while Mike's crew was like being stuck in the drug-fueled, free love 1960s. Doug's crew was like being transported into an episode of *The Sopranos*.

The motel we stayed at was owned by Jim and Michael Hill, and they were the bosses of Denver. They played poker, they played gin, they drank, and they always had some mean-looking mob guys around. Jimmy was a big-time pot farmer in addition to owning the motel and a few other business ventures in Denver. It was Jimmy who took me under his wing after I lost twelve hundred bucks to him in a game of gin and couldn't pay. It was Jim who I would eventually partner with in a dinner boat venture in Seattle. But that would be later, much later.

With Doug's crew, we traveled. We hit the East Coast for a while, and milked those grounds as much as we could. And Mike Furhman had been right about Doug's crew: it was small and inexperienced. I was the permanent driver once I got there, and after traveling with Doug and demonstrating my knowledge and leadership, I gained his trust and the trust of the owners. I was in Las Vegas when they decided to reward me for my hard work.

"Greg, come on up here!" Doug said, standing in the middle of the room. "Hey, make room for Greg."

The guys parted, and I made my way to the center of the motel conference room.

"I'm not much for speeches, so I'll just get right to it," Doug said. "Greg, you've been an asset to this company. You've been an excellent leader, a great motivator, and an exemplary employee. And because of your dedication, hard work, and loyalty, you have earned your own crew. "

Everything I had worked so hard for came to fruition that afternoon. I now had my own crew and I could forge my own destiny. It was now all within my reach. My income now depended on me. It depended on how hard I worked, how well I trained my crew, and how great of a leader I was. They gave me three guys to start with, and the rest was now up to me.

The beginning was rough, like any new venture starting out. We postdated checks, we juggled money, we hustled, scraped, and clawed our way through those early months. Once I started to get a little breathing room, however, I hired a guy name Bill Gillespie. Bill was a guy who would become one of my best friends and who would help me change the business. Bill stayed by my side through the ups and downs and who remained my partner up until just a couple of years ago. Bill mattered in my life.

We grew. My crew grew, and I helped Mecca grow. And things were good, at least until Joe grew tired of Doug's sales practices. Back in those days, you didn't travel with rival sales crews. Doug loved to travel with his buddies from Tipco. And so the split came. The final straw was when Mike Furhman offered Doug a lot more money than Joe would pay if Doug came over to Tipco and brought his crew with him. And that was that; Doug left. And I left with him. I owed my loyalty to Doug, and so my decision had been an easy one. I got to keep my money and my position. I answered to Doug, who answered to his buddy Mike Furhman. Being under Doug, and not working directly under Mike, insulated my guys from falling into the drug-fueled orbit that surrounded the rest of the crews at Tipco. And by doing it this way, we were able to really stay focused and really make money. Times were good, at least until it was time for that year's Fourth of July vacation at the Lake of the Ozarks. That July, everything was put back into perspective for me.

As a crew manager, I had a primo cabin right on the lake near the dock. There was this kid who wanted to go swimming. That's all he talked about on the way up to the lake . . . diving right in and going for a swim. I remember walking out of my cabin and actually seeing him jump off of the dock. He was ecstatic about being at the lake, and so was everyone else. It was party time.

I watched as his arm came up out of the water, and then go back under, and instantly, I knew something was wrong. Without hesitation, I dove into the water and began searching for him. I stayed down until my lungs felt as if they were about to burst, and then came up for a breath and went right back beneath the surface of the water. I searched for this kid, and searched for him, and did everything that I could to find him. I gave up out of bone-deep exhaustion. He was the first kid I ever lost on the road.

The sheriff's department came out and subsequently found him. I didn't know that when someone drowns they don't sink; they float near the surface of the water. I was diving too deep in my search for him. There were two hundred kids at the lake that day, and none of us had known what to do. I thought about that day for a long time; in fact, I still think about it sometimes. I wanted to save him, I wanted to . . . I can still see his face, I can still see the joy on his face, his smile . . . He wanted to swim and unwind and have fun, and me, I just wanted to save him. Needless to say, we never went back to the Lake of the Ozarks after that. I still haven't returned even to this day.

I needed to unwind after the tragedy at the lake. I found myself heading back to the comforts of home. I needed to be near family. I needed to be near the familiar. My need for peace turned into a game of Twenty Questions with my father and my siblings.

"When are you going to come home and go to college?" Dad asked.

We stood in the backyard on the patio while Dad was working on the grill.

"I'm not going to come home and go to college," I answered. "Why not?" he asked. "Haven't you gotten this out of your system yet?"

"Dad, this is not something that I needed to get out of my system!" I replied. "This is what I do. It's what I do for a living. It's what I'm going to do for a living."

My father shook his head in disapproval.

"Dad, I'm good at it," I told him, pleading my case. "I'm a manager. I have a crew of people that I'm responsible for. They depend on me, and I take care of them. I motivate my team, we plan, we go out, and we execute. And we're good, we're really good. I can make it in the industry."

"Yeah, but don't you think you should at least go to college so you'll have something to fall back on?" he asked. "Something respectable?"

And that was when I knew what was bothering him. It was no secret how my siblings viewed my job. They were college graduates, making their way through the corporate world, climbing up in society—while they viewed what I did as akin to being a street urchin.

"Dad, I'm sorry, but I'll never be Rotary Club material," I told him. "I'll never be like Mike, or Maureen, or Beth, or Patsy. I'll never be Mr. Tucson, or chairman of the bank, or president of the board. And I don't want a backup plan. I don't want a backup plan, because I'm not going to fail, and I'm never going to give up. That's what you instilled in me, Dad. You taught us all to never give up. I'm never going to give up, and I'm never going to let down all of the people who are depending on me. Take care of the troops, Dad. Don't make excuses. If you want something done, do it. Those are the lessons you taught us."

I watched my dad stand a little taller and take measure of me. I saw something in his eyes that I thought was only reserved for my brother Mike. My dad was proud of me.

We never had that conversation again. In fact, it was right after that, that my father called Doug and asked him what I needed to succeed. Doug told him that I could use a couple of reliable transports. My father surprised me one day by taking me out to look at some Suburbans. He wanted to buy me two of them. The only reason he never got around to it is because I left town shortly afterward, and he suffered a massive stroke. The stroke left Dad paralyzed on his left side. I later found out that even before we had our conversation in the yard, Dad used to defend me whenever my brothers and sisters would be talking about my career choice. He would recite the cost of a college tuition, which he paid for all of them, and then point out the fact that I had never asked him for anything. My father had always been proud of my independence and the fact that I was making my own way through life. Dad had always been strong and independent, and he saw that part of himself in me.

I returned to get my crew together and hit the road again after Dad started to recover from his stroke. Things were happening, and the industry was changing and growing rapidly. In fact, it was about this time when Tipco closed its doors, and Mike Furhman and his partner Belo Kellum started TICOA, which stood for Trans International Clearing of America. Doug joined the company as a manager, and so did I.

With this new crew, we traveled the East Coast. Doug's crew grew over time, and he needed reliable, experienced people to manage the newcomers. I was in Las Vegas when I got the news that I was being promoted.

"May I have everyone's attention please?" Doug shouted. We were in a hotel conference room on the seedy side of Vegas. It was not the kind of hotels that the tourists stayed in when coming to the city, but rather the kind that could be rented by the hour. We had rented a good share of rooms for our stay there.

"Attention!" Doug called out again, lifting his hand into the air to simmer the buzzing sound swirling throughout the room from all of the chitter-chatter. "I have an announcement to make."

The buzz in the room died down, and soon, everyone's attention was focused on Doug.

"We've grown a lot this past year," Doug told those gathered. "We've expanded, had some success, experienced some growing pains, but we've made it through. We're now looking forward to an even better year, and even bigger growth!"

Applause went around the room.

"A big part of our growth is owed to a guy that works as hard as three people," Doug continued. "He came over with me from another company, and his experience has been invaluable. Here at TICOA, we believe in rewarding hard work, experience, and loyalty. We are always watching. We may not say anything, but trust me, we take note of the people who go that extra mile, the people who work hard, demonstrate leadership, and great salesmanship. This guy demonstrated all of those qualities. Greg, come on up here!"

Applause went throughout the room.

I made my way up toward the front to where Doug was standing. He wrapped his arm around me and pulled me to his side.

"Meet, TICOA's newest crew manager!" Doug announced. Again, raucous applause erupted. And just like that, I was on my way up.

My newfound position came with zero dollars. They did, however, give me a crew of three to get me started. They sent me to Omaha first, and we worked that area as best we could. It was a struggle at first. We juggled money, we postdated checks, we did everything that we could to survive. We squeezed every dollar that we could out of Omaha, and worked our way down to Denver. It was in Denver where I met two people who would become long-term partners and central figures in my life. The first of those people was Jim Hill.

Like I mentioned before, Jim and his brother Michael were considered the bosses of Denver. Jim was a big time pot farmer with deep connections to the underworld. That they were mob guys was an open-and-unspoken secret. It was Jimmy who took me under his wing after I lost $1,200 to him in a game of gin. He knew that I couldn't pay, and rubbing me out would have been a waste of a bullet. So Jim did the next best thing; he pulled me in and decided to teach me everything that he knew.

I appreciated Jim for everything that he taught me. I learned a lot from he and Bill Gillespie. Both men would play a major part in my life. Bill would eventually become my business partner, and even today, Bill is still one of my closest friends.

My crew slowly grew. We called ourselves the Superstars. Every crew had a name. It was done to create an esprit de corps, and to foster friendly competition among the crews. Eventually, the money started to come, and I found a way to get a hold of a vehicle. Our first crew vehicle was an old Lincoln. While the other more established crews would be riding around in brand-new minivans and Suburbans, my crews rolled around in old Lincolns, old Mercury Marquises, and old Granadas. We weren't as glamorous as the other crews, but we were hard chargers. I turned my crew into a group of sales sharks. If you answered the door, we were going to close the deal.

It was during this time when an old crew guy named Jerry came back around. He wanted back in, and none of the other crews wanted him. I took him. Taking Jerry in was one of the best decisions I ever made. With his age came experience, and Jerry was happy to share with me everything that he knew. And he knew a lot. He was like a living, breathing encyclopedia of door-to-door sales. He knew where the money was, and he knew how to squeeze every last drop out of an area. He was legendary.

Jerry was a gruff, one-eyed, scruffy old fellow. He reminded me of the trainer from Rocky. He had this method for building a successful team. He would bring over these kids from England. They wanted little, and their English accents guaranteed the sale. Something about a British accent that conveyed trust, intelligence, and honesty. If the Brits were selling it, then it must be great, right? Right! At least it was right on my end, and right for my bottom line. My crew kept growing and growing, until I had more than thirty kids working for me. Money was pouring in so fast, that I bought us a limo.

Belo Kellum sold me his limousine, and I hired this kid named Jeff, who was the brother of one of the girls on my crew, to be my driver. The limo was more than just an ego trip for me; it was a motivational tool for my crew. One, it showed them what they could one day accomplish, and two, the reward for a good day's sales would be to take the limo for a night out drinking with the boss. I absolutely loved taking the kids out in the limo, and they got a big kick out of it as well. We would even take the limo up to Mount Rushmore. There was a wonderful fishing spot behind the mountain that we would go to. As a matter of fact, we would take the limo up to Montana, Idaho, as well as South Dakota, and fish out of the roof. They were great times. The money was coming in, the kids were making money and traveling, and TICOA was growing by leaps and bounds.

I always tried to do the right thing, and I tried hard to be a good boss. I would read *Think and Grow Rich* to my crews to try to motivate them. I always thought that inspiration was a greater motivating factor than fear. I knew that there existed two types of leaders: those like Rick who used fear, and the type that I wanted to be. I was determined to be better than Rick, better than all of those who were in charge when I came into the industry. I wanted my kids to do well, not just for me, but so they could succeed. I wanted to give them all of the things that Rick never gave me. And chief among those things was a real shot at success.

CHAPTER 4

⌾══╾⌾

We primarily worked the West Coast during the winter because the weather was better. I had my crew hitting California hard in those days, because it truly was the land of milk and honey. We made sale after sale, propelling our way toward phenomenal growth. We were expanding so much, so fast that I had newcomers recruiting newcomers; everybody wanted to be part of the crew. And fortunately for me, things worked out this way. One of the kids on my crew knocked on a door in San Jose one day, and met this girl name Andrea Prince. Andrea was on vacation from a company that sold concentrated cleaners. He gave her a great sales pitch and recruited her. He passed along my number and got her for me. I called her, and the rest was history. I picked Andrea up in my white Mercedes 450 SEL and took her out on a date. My fancy car and giant brick of a cell phone impressed her enough for her to join my crew, but it was my smile that won her heart. I picked Andrea up for an interview and took her to San Francisco to get her drunk and have sex with her, but she would have no parts of it. Fortunately, she still decided to go on the road with me. Eventually Andrea did decide to go on a date with me, but she made me wait three months before accepting my offer for a date.

Andrea was an excellent salesperson, and wound up being my top salesperson and eventually got her own crew. She was a great motivator, so much so, that she took the kids that I was going to fire and turned them into great salespeople. Andrea was a true partner, a great friend, and an enormous asset to the company. She meant so much to me, that I eventually married her.

It was about this time that my friend and mentor, Jim, decided to close up shop in Denver and move up to Seattle. Jim bought the Silver Swan, a really famous converted 1920s mail boat and converted it into a dinner boat. The Silver Swan was the last of the famed Mosquito Fleet, which were the boats that delivered mail and food to all the islands around Seattle. The fleet had also transported dock workers during World War II to the Bremerton Shipyards. Jim had this great idea that he would fix up this historic old boat and take people out on the water for dinner. Seattle was paradise to Jimmy. The weather was different: the people were different . . . The entire environment was different. You would have thought Jimmy had discovered his Shangri-la, and in some ways, I guess he did. And the thing about Jimmy was that when he found a good thing, he wanted to let you know that he would do a good thing. He wouldn't let up about me coming out to Seattle and going into the dinner boat business with him. Seattle seemed like a really nice place to settle down, and I really wanted to have a life somewhere. I was making money hand over foot, and I needed to invest in something. The way Jim described it, was that we could put on tuxedos and be a part of great events in people's lives. As a bonus, there would also be great jazz music, and great food.

Jimmy got his hands on some credit card forms for the dinner boat. My crew started using them to take credit card orders for our magazine sales. People would use their credit cards, and this would feed the bank account that Jimmy used to fix up the boat once we became partners. I was happy, because I was finally able to stay in Seattle with Jimmy and help rebuild and become a part of his dream. His dream, actually became my dream. In fact, I enjoyed being on the water so much, that I decided that I actually wanted to live on a boat.

The cool thing about shopping for a boat is that people take you out on boat rides to try them out. So my crew and I started going out on these wonderful boat rides.

Eventually I did buy a boat. It was a houseboat. This was separate from the dinner boat. I put a bunch of mattresses on it, and the crew and I lived on the houseboat. I bought the thing from an old lady named Blanche. I learned from Blanche that an 85 year old lady will put it to you worse than a 25 year old. Sweet old ladies are the one you have to look out for when doing a business deal. Blanche knew that she had a rookie and she stuck it to me on the deal. I knew absolutely nothing about boats, and it showed. I begin to fix up my houseboat, and I put in a regular toilet, the wrong plumbing, and the wrong electrical systems. Needless to say, my houseboat was always flooding and catching fire. Whenever someone would take a shower, the boat would shock the shit out of them. It wasn't until I met this guy who helped me fix it up that I was able to get the boat done the right way.

In the magazine business, things ebbed and flowed. Prosperity was cyclical. I lost most of my crew when they all started smoking crack. Others moved on because they couldn't take living on the houseboat on the delta in Stockton, California. In a way, I don't blame them. The dock where we lived was called Turd Alley, because only the lowest of the low docked and lived there. Eventually, it was only Andrea and I left. I had to go back up to Seattle and hook up with Bill and rebuild my crew with some of his guys. The guys Bill gave me were primo, and it took no time to get things back on track. We went out on the road and spent about two weeks in each city that we hit, and in no time, I was back in Seattle renting a nice house for me and Andrea to lay our heads in.

Just when things were starting to go smoothly, like clockwork, life intervened. Bill had a girlfriend who he really liked name Julie. But Julie secretly started dating one of Bill's junior managers. Naturally, when Bill found out, he wasn't too pleased with either of them. They still worked for Bill, so he made it not a nice place to be for the two of them. This gave Furhman the opportunity to get back at Bill. He absolutely hated Bill, because Bill had slept with this new girl that Furhmann had asked him not to sleep with. Bill ended up having sex with her in the stairwell of a Holiday Inn on her second day on the job, so he was furious. He offered to sell me his company, but only if I messed over Bill and not brought him over with me. Naturally, I refused. Bill had always been loyal to me, and so I was going to be loyal to Bill. A month later, Furhman cut a deal with Bill's girlfriend and the junior manager she was sleeping with, and brought them over to TICOA and made both of them senior managers. Bill was devastated.

I told Bill to bring his crew up to Seattle and get some rest. I then called up Mike Furhman and told him what I thought about what he had done. Mike didn't deny doing it, or the reason for doing it. He hated Bill. I told him that if he would do it to Bill, he would do the same to me and Andrea. He didn't deny that he could do something like that again, so I made it clear to him that our relationship was over. It was hard breaking ties with Furhmann, he had been my boss, my mentor, and my friend. After what he did, I told him that I didn't that that we could even be friends anymore.

The magazine business in those days was really segregated. The black crews kept to themselves and hired only black, and the white crews did the same. Actually, the White crews did do some mixing, but for the most part, the Black crews were wholly Black. This guy named Joe Edge owned Mecca, which was the central clearinghouse. The clearinghouse got the magazines from the publishers, and supplied them to us, the secondary market. Mecca dealt with Pennington, which was a white crew. The publishers also dealt with black crews run by Don Scott and Bob Lake. Bob Lake actually owned the clearinghouse. Don ran the biggest black crew. All of his people were black. His managers were black, his wife was black, and his cars and dogs were black. The thing about Don's crew was that he was able to hire as many people as he wanted. Unemployment was high across the country, and the unemployment rate was even higher in the black community, so Don had his pick of hard workers. And in order to keep your job under Don, you had to bust your ass. Don was the king of the magazine business.

I hooked up with my partner Bill, and we went to see Don Scott, and ask him if he would clear for us. In other words, we wanted him to supply us with our maga... with Don started out good, with them sho... and yachts, and this giant shiny new office bu... were housed in, but we still left feeling uneasy. P... to Michigan City to kiss Don's ass, we flew to ... ...J to pick up a bunch of orders and checks for orde... ...at Bill had submitted for us to the company we used to work for. Afterward, we flew to Seattle to officially open up our own company. Bill's uncle, Ken Frick, flew up to Seattle to help us get things set up. Ken rented an office, and then bought a bunch of used office equipment from a bankruptcy sale at an air-conditioning company. We called the company Pacific Coast Clearing Company. We hired Bill's mom, Nancy, as our customer service rep. We hired a secretary name Sue Smith, and we were able to talk a friend of ours named Norma to leave TICOA and move up to Seattle and enter the orders for us.

PCC was going to be part of a new era of change in the magazine business. Kids were still getting beaten, threatened, and left stranded out on the road. We were going to change all of that. We were going to professionalize the magazine business. Ken was just the guy to do it. He was honest, straitlaced, and business-minded. We made Ken the CEO.

After setting things up in Seattle, we flew to see Don, to see if he would fill the orders that we already had, which we picked up from San Antonio. Needless to say, that trip did not go well. Don basically wanted to extort us. The numbers he presented were highway robbery, and to top it off, he knew that we had orders that needed to be filled and checks for those orders that had already been cashed. Don laid it out pretty clear: we would clear through him, or we would go to jail for fraud. It was our taste of the business world. The *real* business world. We had to let Don think that he was going to eat our lunch and that we were going to smile while he did it. After spending a day with Don, we knew that we would basically be jumping from the frying pan and into the fire. We took our orders back to Seattle with us.

Ken went back out on the road to drum up some cash and eventually ran into these guys from Clearwater, Florida with a company named Subco. They were phone guys, and they were a huge company. So huge in fact, that they bought a huge mall, cleared it out, and turned it into their phone bank. The guy who owned Subco, started out selling magazines from his kitchen table using numbers out of a phone book. Now, they were moving magazines in the hundreds of thousands and had access to magazines in bulk. His was the king of the magazine phone business, and these guys were the alternative that we had been hoping for. For the first time since being in the business, I had found someone who didn't go through Bob, or Joe, or Don. These guys changed the magazine business. And they were just what I had been looking for.

My big break was followed up by another big move. I had opened up the company office in Seattle for a reason. I had my dinner boat cruises with Jim, and I was also going to make another significant investment as well. After years of calling various motel rooms home, I decided that it was time to plant roots. My dinner boat operation was in Seattle, my magazine company was now in Seattle, so it was time for me to buy a house in Seattle.

I partnered with Bill and bought a house on Fox Island. It was a beautiful home deep in the forest and right on the water.

When the tide went out, you could walk on the beach and pick up clams. It was the most beautiful place I had ever seen, and I spent many moonlit nights walking that gorgeous beach. It helped me to clear my head. Eventually, we would move the dinner boat from Seattle to Tacoma. We set ourselves up out of Gig Harbor. The city of Tacoma had offered to give us a dock because they didn't have any dinner boats there. Needless to say, we jumped at the opportunity.

Opportunities in the Pacific Northwest were abundant. The money was flowing, so I decided to diversify a little. I bought into Baby Sunglasses and invested money into a company that invented beach thongs that stick to your feet without straps. I put money into all kinds of places, thinking that one of them was going to be the big score. I even took to the road to help promote some of my ventures.

I had a friend named Jason who hailed from the sunny, tropical state of Hawaii. Jason convinced me that Hawaii was the market for baby sunglasses and strapless beach thongs, so I flew out with him to promote these businesses. We arrived in Hawaii kind of late in the evening and took a cab out to Jason's mom's house. Andrea was bone-tired, so she took up an offer to lie down and instantly fell asleep. That left me and Jason with time to explore.

The plan was to get to the island, find a nice motel to use as a base for our operations, and then get out and promote. We ventured out to find said motel, and then wound up going to see Jason's old band. It was with these guys that everything in my life changed. We went into a motel parking lot and took hits of ice.

I was gone.

I had been told that ice was a miracle drug, that it would wake me up, give me energy, help me to focus. It was all bullshit, of course, but I bit. For the next three days, I found myself traveling all over Hawaii with a band, smoking crystal meth. Worst of all, everyone in Hawaii was doing it, and everyone thought that it wasn't addictive, and they all thought that there were no harmful side effects. What I saw was that for three days, no one moved from the spot where they were sitting, and that everyone was completely addicted. I knew that Hawaii was in a lot of trouble. And speaking of trouble, once I finally got back to Andrea three days later, I knew that *I* was in a lot of trouble. I lied and told her that I had a spiritual experience. And to put the icing on the cake and get my ass out of the sling, I proposed to her. I left Hawaii a completely different person than I was when I arrived. I now had a monkey on my back.

Back on the mainland, I had dinner cruises running out of Tacoma, while Ken was running the magazine crews out of Seattle. The company was doing good, Bill was doing great, and all of the managers and kids out in the field were doing good as well. Bill was taking the kids up and down the West Coast, and even venturing out to Hawaii, Alaska, and Guam. At least, until they got kicked out of Guam. We ended up being the largest cash field company in the country. We had over 400 kids and thirty sales managers. Everything was going great . . .

At least until I was summoned by the IRS for an audit.

My wonderful meeting with the Internal Revenue Service took place in good old San Antonio. I walked into the IRS offices with an attorney that I had hired through prepaid legal services, and I walked out of that audit owing the federal government over half a million dollars! To say that the auditors that I had were bloodsuckers would be an insult to bloodsuckers everywhere. They wanted me to pay the government $20,000 a month, they wanted to seize my beautiful home on Fox Island, they wanted my dinner boat—they wanted *everything*. I just remember saying no to them. Saying no to everything, I got up, walked out of that meeting, not knowing what I was going to do or how things were going to turn out. All I knew was that I would be damned if I was going to let them take everything I had built away from me. They wanted more from me than what I owed them in taxes. I flew home to Seattle that same evening.

PCC started kicking butt, but that still didn't alleviate my problems with the IRS. To make matter worse, Jimmy got sick, which left the dinner boat operations on my shoulders. I couldn't concentrate on the dinner boat, the magazine business, and my tax problems all at once, so I brought my sister Heather and her husband up to Seattle to run the dinner boat operations. We had named it the Silver Swan Dinner Boat Company, and it was doing pretty well. By doing well, I meant when my sister and her husband Mark weren't at each other's throats. My sister had stopped doing heroin, but she never quite got over her substance abuse. Heather was still a very heavy drinker. Her days in Seattle consisted of running the dinner boat, drinking heavily, and fighting with Mark. Jimmy's arthritis got so bad that he called it quits in Seattle. He packed up and moved back down to Denver so that his sister could take care of him. I bought him out, and sent him away with my love and gratitude.

The magazine business was booming at this time as well. We were getting people from all over the country who had

Silver Swan Dinner Boat

been screwed over by other magazine companies. And these were great salespeople with tons of experience. We expanded like crazy. Ken, Bill, and I went to a motivational seminar, and these guys helped us with our expansion a great deal. They examined our company and reorganized it from top to bottom, helping us to deal with the growth, as well as making sure we were able to squeeze every dollar of potential profit out of the business.

My IRS problems came to a head, and once again, the great days were brought back down to earth by some mystical force that hated to see me doing well. I walked into my attorney's office to see what "great deal" he had struck with the Internal Revenue Service, only to find out that they wanted to give me $1,500 a month to live on, while they take the rest. They wanted my house and everything else I owned. On top of that, they were still asking for $20,000 a month for the next five years. I told them to go to hell. I wasn't going to kill myself working for the IRS for the next five years. I told them that I would simply quit working, and they told me that I couldn't quit working. Again, my answer was no, and I got up and walked out of that meeting as well.

My troubles with the IRS were compounded by the fact that the dinner boat had obtained a liquor license. This, in turn, gave me license to get drunk all of the time. I would go out on the dinner boat . . . and come back in completely wasted. It was then when, for the first time in my life, I contemplated suicide. Either blowing my brains out or running away to some South American country. I didn't have the money to pay the IRS back. I hadn't made the money that they claimed I had made. I figured that all of my troubles would be over with a quick flash of a muzzle.

CHAPTER 5

Things changed after the IRS audit. The fun was gone. Being young, living on Fox Island, running around living carefree, and having money in my pocket was not enough anymore. Bill was gone all of the time, and the reorganization of the company had turned it into something more corporate than I was used to. I had never been comfortable in a corporate environment. For me, the business had always been about hitting the streets, going door-to-door, and making sales. I didn't recognize my own company anymore, and it felt like I no longer belonged there. The feeling that I had in my youth, the feeling that I had of somehow being left behind, once again crept up. I didn't know where I needed to go, but Seattle was the place where I knew that I needed to leave.

My foot out the door was compounded when the Coast Guard pulled the permit on my dinner boat. This left the boat sitting on the dock in my backyard on Fox Island. I had my old houseboat and my Jet Ski moved to my home on Fox Island as well. I would walk out of my back door and stare at them. They looked like boats to most, but to me, they looked like docked dreams. The beautiful view that I once beheld was not blocked by a rusting houseboat, and a way-past-its-prime mail boat from the Mosquito Fleet. With each passing day, Seattle was closing in on me. With each passing day, my life, like the weather, seemed to grow drearier and drearier. I needed to get out. My out came soon enough.

Arizona had never been sailing country, and I had never been a boat guy, so growing up, I was never taught the ins and outs of boating and dock maintenance. No one ever told me that when the power went out due to a storm, you had to manually reset the power on the boat. After one particularly bad storm ravaged the coast, my dinner boat sank. You would have thought that the Exon Valdez had sunk in my backyard. I had the Department of Fisheries, the United States Coast Guard, the Bureau of Land Management, and the Bureau of Indian Affairs all crawling up my ass. They all threatened to put me in prison if it sank again. I tried to get rid of the boat, but no one wanted it. Eventually, I had the last of the Mosquito Fleet boats hauled to the other side of the dock and cut up. That was the end of the swan, the end of an era, and the end of my time in Seattle. I turned over my house to my partner Bill, and then I called up Andrea who was in Tucson planning our wedding, and asked her if she wanted to move to Vegas. Her yes was all it took. I packed up my Harley, our clothing, and the Dobermans, and moved to Las Vegas the next day.

The move to Vegas hadn't been thought out very well. When I got there, I was living in a hotel. But I knew that Andrea deserved better. She had given up her island home in

Seattle, and she deserved better than a hotel room. We went to see a real estate agent the next day. To my surprise, the agent had a picture of Gig Harbor on her wall. The picture sparked a conversation, which culminated in her asking where we wanted to live. We had no idea. She told us that she was planning on moving in with her daughter, and that she had a house on Sahara that she was willing to rent to us. We accepted, and just like that, we moved into our first home in Las Vegas.

Vegas was the change that I had been looking for. It was the complete opposite of Seattle. The sun felt good. The warm weather, the desert landscape, the glitzy hotels—it was all different. I felt fresh and renewed. Reinvigorated even. I hit the road with a new crew to get my mojo back and to see if I could come up with enough cash to get the IRS off of my back. I headed for the East Coast.

My East Coast mojo came back in full force. I built my crew back up and started making really good money again. We traveled up and down the East Coast, working it for all it was worth. And the milk sure was flowing. We took the kids to Boston every year for the Fourth of July. It was during one of these trips to Boston when I got a phone call from Seattle.

"Hey, Greg, there's been an accident," the voice on the other end of the line said.

"Bill, what's the matter?" I asked. "I need you to get up to Seattle."

"Sure," I said. "I'll catch the first flight out." "Great," Bill said. "See you soon."

"Hey, is everything okay?"

"We'll talk about it when you get here."

The thing that we had to talk about was the fact that his new girlfriend's son burned my boat down to ashes. The worse news, was that he had not just burned down my boat, and my dock, but he had managed to burn down all of the boats and all of the docks on the entire island! The kid had been playing with fireworks and accidently lit up the boat, and then the dock, and then the other docks, and then my neighbors' boats. It had been a complete disaster.

I apologized profusely to all of my neighbors. Needless to say, they weren't too receptive to my overtures. And these were the types of people who you didn't want to make enemies of. One of my neighbors was the CEO if Weyerhaeuser, the world's largest privately owned timber company. My neighbor on the other side was the former governor of the State of Washington.

"Well, we're still up in the air," my neighbor said.

"Up in the air?" I asked, lifting an eyebrow.

"Yep," he said nodding. "We're still trying to decide if we're gonna let you live here."

"Let me live here?" I asked incredulously. "I own my house!"

"You think that means anything?" he asked, before turning and walking off.

And I knew that he meant it. It was the first time I really understood what true power meant. Ownership or not, collectively, they had the power to decide my fate. I left Seattle and flew back to Vegas. If they wanted that house, they could fight Bill for it.

Andrea and I had been in Vegas for some time now, and it was time to buy our own place instead of renting from the real estate agent. We found a perfect little house on Ford Road, in what was a new area of town back then. It was the perfect setup, with plenty of room for us to grow. But the room to grow was always taken up by out-of-town guests. When people know that you live in Vegas, they all want to come and visit you once a year. They all want to go to the same shows, they all want to stay out all night, and they all want to experience the "Las Vegas lifestyle." And they never seemed to realize that someone had just left the week before, and that you had just done the exact same thing. It was never-ending traffic. Eventually, it got so bad that we had friends of friends coming and staying in our guest house.

When not constantly entertaining out-of-town guests, Andrea and I had taken to playing Keno, and brunch, and taking in shows like *New York, New York.* I eventually found my way to a hobby that was much more addicting, one that would change my life forever. I eventually starting going to boxing matches.

It was at a boxing event where I met this small-time boxing promoter named Tony. It was Tony who shared with me that fact that all you needed to do to become a boxing manager was fill out a form and sign your name on the dotted line. That was it. That and fifty bucks. I met this promoter named Jimmy Finn at a fight one night, who I was really impressed with. Jimmy was this redheaded Irish guy with a personality that was three times bigger than he was. It was Jimmy who finally convinced me to get into the boxing business. I paid my fifty bucks, filled out the form, and became a licensed boxing manager. Shortly after that, I met Laura Skinner, this awesome Muay Thai fighter from Australia. I convinced her to let me manage her, and she became my first boxer.

Laura moved in with me, and so did Jimmy. We practiced at Richard Steele's gym, which is where I met Roger Mayweather.

Roger and I hit it off instantly. I learned so much from Roger, he even introduced me to Floyd Mayweather Sr., who became a trainer for me. I was quickly immersed into the world of boxing.

The world of Las Vegas boxing was a small one. Everyone knew everyone, and we were all interconnected. Fighters trained together, trainers moved around, managers got boxers and lost boxers, and the world revolved around the gym. Being that I had a little money, I was able to attract some pretty good fighters. I even managed to land a pretty notable fighter in the world of female boxing. Her name was Laura Serrano. I was introduced to Laura Serrano after Laura Skinner hurt her shoulder and moved back to Australia. Jimmy Finn introduced us, and we hit it off instantly. Laura was trained by none other than boxing legend Julio César Chávez. She was an awesome fighter. We called her "Little Chávez." I was able to land her because she had blown her Achilles' tendon. But if anyone knew the power of redemption, it was me. I sent Laura to Mexico to have her tendon operated on and repaired, and had Dr. Voy do the rehab on her once she got back.

The other thing about Las Vegas boxing is that it was heavily connected to the underworld. A lot of these guys would show up from Denver, and they would come in and get Super Bowl seats, comped suites at The Sahara—free everything. They needed a way to get around town, and that was where I came in. One of my managers in the magazine business had a brother named Pete that lived in Vegas. Pete started driving my limo, and eventually we started a limo business together, which was huge in Vegas at the time. It was called Pete's Fleet. And, naturally, we got all the mob business. Pete and I also got into

World Champion Susie Taylor

Champions Maricha Sjaw & Laura Serrano

World Champion Hector Macho Camacho

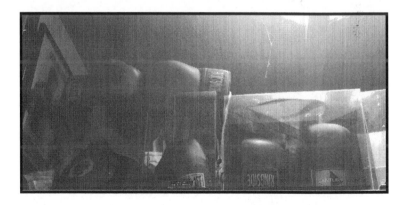

World Champion Bones Adam

World Champion Johnny Tapia

Team Tua

Julio Cesar Chavez & Bill Gillespie

Macho Camacho & Tony from The Car Lot

Team Adams

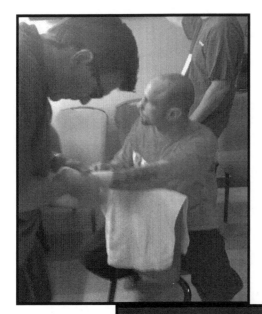

Bones Adams

Bones Adams

Sugar Ray Leonard & Greg Hannley

Trevor McCumbly

the pigeon eradication business, and we even started a meat company together, called Pete's Meats. Wherever there was a dollar to be made, we tried to make it. Pete also introduced me to Randy, the guy who would eventually become my crack dealer. Needless to say, none of my business ventures with Pete ever panned out. Pete got drunk and hit a guy on a bike, and that ended the limo company.

My business ventures with shadowy characters eventually led me into the mortgage industry. I was out playing golf one day, and I got a call saying that this wonderful house was for sale. At the time, I only had about fifty grand, but the real estate agent insisted that this was a deal that I couldn't pass up. I wrote her a check for $50,000, thinking that I could get the loan done, get an appraisal, and pay off the loan. The only guys that would do it was this mortgage company called Valley Pine Mortgage out of Baltimore. Mike Matalone's girlfriend worked for them. He owed me a lot of money. I told him that I would forgive his debt if he could get her to get her mortgage company to finance me. They were hard money loan guys who I convinced to give me a three-hundred-fifty-thousand-dollar loan, even though the owner wouldn't allow an appraiser to come onto the property. Once I saw what they could do, I wanted to go into business with them. They did my loan, and I convinced them that we could sell a lot of mortgages in Vegas, so we went into business together. We opened a mortgage company called Valley Pine Mortgages. I would get the loan packages together, and then fly to Baltimore to see if they could do the loans. Eventually, we got a cease-and-desist order from the state, so I asked them to get a license to do mortgages in Vegas.

Problem solved.

The huge house that I bought turned out to be pretty freaking awesome. It was completely self-sufficient with its own water catchment, its own generators, and with its own underground cooling system. The main house was 16,000 square feet, with a 3500-square foot underground house. They wanted $250K for the house, which was a steal. The reason for it being so cheap was because the guy who was building it was killed while building the well. A chain snapped and cut him in half. His spirit was known as the ghost of Prince Ranch. His widow was left living alone in the underground house by herself on the edge of Vegas, and she was ready to get rid of it.

The house was this enormous white building that looked more like a church or a school, and a giant house. It had these enormous white towers, and the entire house was completely open on the inside. Even the bedrooms had no doors.

The biggest problem with the house was that it was built out of exposed concrete blocks. I knew that in the state that it was in, there was no way that I was going to be able to get it appraised for a decent amount. My solution was to have the block painted, and to bring in thousands of feet of baseboards so that the house looked like it was being done.

About the time of the house purchase, I met this fellow named Josh who owned a small wildlife company. I had this giant ranch that I wasn't living in at the time. I would just go out there and fix it up when I got time, so I told him that he could move his animals out there. Meeting Josh had given me a wonderful idea. I had Josh bring his tiger out to the ranch on the same day it was scheduled for inspection. When the inspector showed up, Josh and I followed him around the house with the tiger. Needless to say, it was probably the quickest inspection in the history of the country. The house ended up being appraised for $600,000. I paid off the original loan and used the rest to fix up the place. The house itself turned out to be a great financial decision. Over the years, I would fix up the house, get it reappraised, pull money out of it, and invest the cash and keep fixing the house up. Eventually, I would go on to sale that house for over $2 million.

The house was more ranch than house. I allowed Josh to build an enclosure on the property and move his tiger and a lion out to the ranch. The inside of the house took the term "open concept" to a whole new level. This enormous house had only two bedrooms on the first floor, and the rest of it was wide open. I started letting Josh bring guys out to the house to practice their magic shows and stuff, and soon, Josh had people calling from all over asking if he had this animal or that. Immediately, I saw money. Josh had a company called Safari Wildlife that did animal shows, and I bought into it, and bought all the new animals. People would request certain animals, and we would go out and buy the animals they wanted. Pretty soon, we had miniature donkeys, miniature horses, miniature bulls, miniature cows, horses, potbellied pigs, kangaroos, chimps, baboons . . . you name it. We brought them all out to the ranch.

I continued my dance with cocaine, delving deeper and deeper into the abyss with each passing day. And with each passing day, I watched my life grow weirder and weirder. The second floor of my house had two big hallways and a long gantry way where one could stand upstairs and look down over the railing onto the first floor. I remember standing up there and looking down into the open area of the first floor and seeing a photo shoot with a bunch of models on one side of the room, and the tiger on the other side of the room staring at a little person dressed like Charlie Chaplin riding the miniature horse around the living room. The tiger was licking his chops and visualizing a nice meal out of the little person and the horse. My life had become surreal.

Tarzan the Chimp came to the ranch next. Tarzan was a retired movie chimp from Los Angeles. He would wave at little kids and get them to come closer, and then reach around, grab some poop, and throw it at them. Tarzan also smoked. How he learned, or where he picked up the habit is something I couldn't tell you. All I know is that the first day I met him, he pulled a cigarette and my lighter out of my pocket and fired up the cigarette and smoked it. And then came Merlin the camel. We would take Merlin for walks and he would give you a kiss, and as soon as you turned your head, he would spit on you. And not just regular spit, but nasty, giant camel loogies. Yes, my life had become that surreal.

Having this show crowd around me all of the time meant that all kinds of people were traipsing through the ranch. I met people from everywhere. I met many people in the animal world who really didn't take very good care of their animals. Soon, people started bringing me animals to care for.

My house in Vegas was 16,000 square foot, and the floors where all concrete. It was cold, bare, unwelcoming, and I was growing tired of looking at the gray floors. While on the road, I learned that Dalton Georgia was the capitol of the carpet world. I called Dalton, Georgia, and pretended to be a carpet guy, and I was able to get $10 a square yard carpet for a dollar a square yard. Needless to say, my house was carpeted beautifully.

Another guy I met in Vegas was Jim Boone. I found Jim while perusing the paper and seeing his add announcing that he did furniture auctions. I called Jim up to see if he would be interested in doing an estate sale at the house. He would stage the furniture like it belonged to the home, and in exchange, I would get paid in furniture. I thought, "What the hell?" My house was pretty much empty, and I could use some free furniture. They filled up my home with this really expensive, drop-dead gorgeous furniture, and set up the sale. And people showed up in droves. The funny thing about it was that as soon as someone purchased some "one of a kind" piece, another was brought out of the garage and put in its place. We held an estate sale every weekend for a few months, and I was able to really fill my house up with some gorgeous pieces of furniture as payment.

My foray into the Vegas boxing world had led me to install a boxing ring, a gym, and a heck of a workout facility at the ranch. My training facility, my license, my roster of fighters, and my boxing club membership meant I was in. I had money and a great facility, and everyone wanted to sell me fighters. I christened my ranch, Prince Ranch, which I named after my wife, whose maiden name had been Prince. It was about this time when I acquired my first legitimate fighter, Bones Adams. Bones would eventually become champion, but that was later. Right now, he was mine. I also met Big Al, who was the first guy to knock out Mike Tyson in an amateur ring. Big Al became my bodyguard.

Being the owner of Prince Ranch trainer facility allowed me to come into contact with all kinds of heavy hitters in the boxing world. I read about this wonderful gentleman name

Eddie Futch, who just so happened to be Jo Frazier's trainer. Eddie was going to be featured in *Esquire* magazine feature titled *Men Over Ninety*, and he had them take the pictures at the ranch. I remember Eddie had this beautiful Swiss wife named Eva at the time. Eddie was the guy who trained me on how to give corner instructions. Eddie and Eva were two of the nicest people I've ever met.

It was about this time when the ranch started getting really famous. The *Esquire* magazine shoot with Eddie put the ranch on a whole new level as the go-to training facility in the world. I was now a mover and shaker in the boxing world, and I would have, at various times, César Chávez, "Macho" Camacho, Wayne McCullough, David Tua, etc., come and stay out at the ranch. Whenever there was a big fight in Vegas, one of the teams would inevitably stay out at the ranch and train. HBO would come out and do interviews and do shows out at the ranch. Prince Ranch slowly began to make noise as the place to stay and train if you were fighting in Vegas.

As crazy as my life was at the time, it got even crazier quickly. I met this guy name Randy, who re-introduced me to coke. So now I had my old friend crack, and my new friend cocaine, both competing for my affection. Never one to like confrontation, I settled the dispute by doing both.

The thing about crack is that when you first smoke it, it rushes over you, and you are forever chasing that initial high. The second hit you take, makes you paranoid. I was constantly walking around or driving around the ranch paranoid, searching for noises and sounds that weren't there. With crack cocaine what you find out is that on day one, everyone is around you. Day two, you're all alone. Day three, you're depressed, and filthy, and you feel like your worth as a human being is gone. And you promise yourself and everyone else that you'll never do it again, and yet, you are constantly searching for it. Once you realize that you've become a crack addict, your whole world changes. Nobody wants to become a crack addict, and the moment that you admit to yourself that you are, is the worst moment of your life.

It was about this time when I met someone who would become one of my closest and dearest friends. His name was Semere.

Semere showed up from Florida with a 120-foot stretch limousine. He was from Eritrea. I don't know how I met Semere. He kinda just showed up. And it was a great thing that he did because I was without a limo at the time. My partner Pete had hit a guy while driving drunk and totaled my other limo.

About the same time Semere showed up was when I met Carla, my second female boxer. Carla was built like a bodybuilder, and she was really pretty. Her dad owned the A/C company that I had contracted to work on the ranch. Carla was a monster in the ring. Pound for pound, she could hit as hard as any male boxer in Vegas at the time.

Moving into my circle at the time was another guy named Chuck. At six foot four, Chuck was a giant of a guy with an even larger personality. I met Chuck through Carla, he was her ex-boyfriend. Initially Chuck wanted to kill me for signing Carla, because she had an aneurism, and he was afraid that she would get killed if she fought. Chuck was this caring guy who always had the most beautiful girlfriends you could imagine, and he was constantly making everyone laugh. One of the best

Semere the Driver

times we ever had was on Halloween, when Chuck dressed up as Robin Hood and was dancing around the casino in these green tights. He would eventually become my go-between with all of the scammers and get-rich business schemers that came through Vegas.

About this time, there was this cast of characters around me. You had Jimmy Finn, the Irish boxing promoter, Chuck the bodybuilder, and Josh the animal trainer, all living at the ranch. And then you had this cast of boxers living out there as well. Susie Taylor came into the mix, T-Bird and Desiree and her kids. Laura Serrano from Mexico was there. You had Rod, this seventy-year-old women's boxing expert who brought along with him thousands of boxing videos for us to use for training. You also had the animals, and last but not least, you had the drugs. I was now using meth and cocaine, as well as smoking pot. You combine meth and wild animals . . . and all sorts of things can go wrong.

Zarina the tiger

Leo the lion

Jagger the tiger & Andrea

Josh, Desire, Andrea & Jagger the tiger

Jagger the tiger & David Tua

Jagger the tiger

Oslon

Susie Taylor and Tarzan

Tarzan

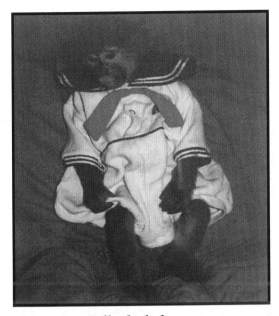

Billy the baboon

Merlin the camel

CHAPTER 6

I came home one day to find a photo shoot taking place in my front yard. They had the lion jumping from one box to another, without a tether or leash on him. The thing about this particular incident was that whenever they fed the lion, they simply walked to his pen with grocery bags and fed him from the bag. Well, we just so happened to be coming back from the grocery store when this particular photo shoot was taking place. Needless to say, things did not go well.

The lion took one look at the grocery bags and instantly thought that it was feeding time. He quickly forgot about the photo shoot and took off after us. Even though I was stoned, I ran for the door faster than I had ever run in my entire life. Luckily, Rod dropped the grocery bag that he was carrying, and the lion went for the bag. A good thing that he did, because in my panic, I didn't open the front door far enough, and the door struck me in the head, knocking me out.

Despite my near-fatal run-in with the lion, I still kept using. I starting smoking even more pot about this time. And by more, I mean *a lot!* I smoked with Tarzan the chimp all the time, because like me, he was a total stoner. We kept it from Josh, because he would have been self-righteous about it. Despite that fact Tarzan would ask for it.

Our animal empire kept expanding, along with my use. We already had the massive Bengal tiger, which my wife brought to my fortieth birthday party and rode, but we managed to get our hands on a gorgeous white tiger named Zarina. We also bought some lion cubs and a bunch of other animals. Of all the animals we had out at the ranch, the massive Bengal tiger was the most volatile. Taking his volatility lightly would later prove fatal.

Josh had owned Jagger the tiger since he was a cub. And Jagger had been performing since he was seven weeks old. He had been in all kinds of ads, shows, and countless motion pictures. He was more famous than most of the boxers that had been to the ranch. He could be the most docile and gentle creature you could ever meet. And sometimes, he would remember that he was a Bengal tiger, and do whatever the hell he wanted. He showed us that on many occasions.

I remember this one time when a buddy of mine was getting married and thought it would be a kick to have Jagger to participate in the wedding. The way things were supposed to work was that Josh was supposed to put the ring on the tiger and have him wait down the aisle. Josh would then call Jagger, and Jagger would be let off of his leash so that he could walk down the aisle to Josh. Josh would then remove the ring and give it to the groom, who would, in turn, give it to his bride.

That was the way it was *supposed* to work. How it actually went down was a different story entirely.

The tiger was tied to a motor home, which he promptly bit the tire off, causing the tire to explode. This should have been the first omen that things weren't going to go right. The second trainer didn't show up, and he was supposed to be the one to manage the tiger while Josh was standing near the groom. Being that it was my buddy's wedding, naturally, I opened my big mouth and volunteered to release the tiger once Josh got his attention and called for him.

Prior to the start of the ceremony, Josh handed me a cup of chicken that was going to be given to Jagger as a reward later. Unbeknownst to me, Jagger was watching me the entire time and saw me set the cup of chicken down on top of this large fifty-gallon ice chest. And even if he hadn't seen me, I'm pretty sure he would have smelled the chicken anyway. Well, the wedding commences, and Josh gives me the signal, and I released the tiger. Jagger immediately ran for the ice chest, ripped the top off, and started roaring and devouring the chicken. He has the ring around his neck, he's devoured the chicken, he now has the ice chest in his mouth shaking it violently, and he's growling and swiping at everyone who approaches him. This was a large ice chest filled to the brim with ice and soda, and Jagger lifted it and shook it like it was nothing. Make a long story short, Josh finally gets the ring from Jagger, races over to the groom, and the minister conducts the fastest wedding ceremony in history. Jagger spent the entire time they were exchanging vows growling at everyone. The wedding party dispersed as soon as the vows were given.

The wedding fiasco should have been a warning to me that things were beginning to spiral out of control. The fact that

Jagger hadn't eaten anyone should have been a wake-up call for me to get my shit straight. Jagger was my tiger; he was the product of a company that I owned half of. Had things gone worse, I could have been sued out the ass, or ended up being charged—or both. I chalked it all up to being lucky, instead of calling it what it really was: an enormous blessing from The Big Man Upstairs. Instead of me counting my blessings and turning my life around, I kept rolling the dice. And the thing about rolling the dice in Vegas is that eventually, everyone loses.

Josh kept bringing more animals out to the ranch. Most of the time, I wouldn't even know what we had, or where they even came from, or when they had arrived. I remember one night waking up to the sound of wolves growling. I knew that I didn't have any wolves on the ranch. I got dressed, went outside, and, of course, it was pitch black out and I couldn't see my hand if I held it in front of my face. So I flip my lighter on—and right in from of me there are twelve Alaskan wolves growling at me from inside an enclosure. Naturally, I get scared and backed away as quickly as I could—only to bump into something behind me. I could feel it was a cage. All of a sudden, I can feel this warmth come over me, and behind me, I hear this heavy breathing. I turned—and there is a massive Kodiak bear inside of the cage behind me. So there is a pack of wolves to the front, and *two* massive Kodiak bears behind me. Unbeknownst to me, this guy's trailer broke down, and Josh let him keep the bears and wolves on the ranch. Did I mention that I had binged out the night before, so I was still tweeking? Things only managed to get worse the next day.

The owner of the bears shows up the next day and goes to let the bears out for a walk. Just my luck, the bears are pissed at each other for some reason, and they ended up engaging in a full-on bear fight. The guy who owned them grabbed the water hose and started spraying them. They weren't having it. I wasn't having any of it either. I climbed as fast as I could, and I watched the entire thing from the top of the bear enclosure. It was the first time I had second thoughts about having all of these animals around. But I had a reputation in Vegas for having my own private zoo, for having world-famous boxers around, for having models around doing photo shoots all of the time. I loved that reputation, and I wasn't ready to give it up. Even if it could eventually cost me—or someone else— their life. I reached into my pocket, pulled out a joint, and fired up. Nothing like watching two massive bears destroy your yard and rile up all of the other animals while getting high as hell. I knew I had a problem, but didn't know how bad it was, nor how to fix it. I was on a train that I didn't know how to get off of.

My business ventures in Vegas continued to grow. I had Prince Ranch, I had the show animals, I still owned Pacific Coast Clearing, I had Valley Pine Mortgage, etc. . . . I got into flipping houses in Vegas, I was talked into starting this flame retardant company called Flame Block, I had a magazine company, I started a car dealership, and I opened up a restaurant called Millennium. Talk about diversification. I went into business with everyone. Times were good, the cash was rolling in, I was on both a natural high and a self-induced one, and my life was on cruise control.

At least I thought so.

My care-free existence came crashing down on me one day when I received a phone call from Freddy, my landscaper at the ranch. He called me to tell me that the photographer has a young girl out at the ranch photographing her and she's pretty naked. The photographer had already been accused of having a relationship with a girl who was fourteen, and if there was one thing that I don't play around with, it's hurting children. I immediately drove out to the photographer's studio and confronted the bastard. The son of a bitch starts telling me how he and the girl had this "connection," and how in love they were. I told him that if I ever heard of him going anywhere near that girl again, I was going to kill him. I also let him know that if he ever comes out to my ranch again, I was going to kill him. The guy never came out to the ranch again. He ended up going to prison for twenty years.

By this time in my life, I had started doing a lot of coke. I would always do it alone, when Andrea wasn't around. And being at home, doing drugs alone, was the loneliest feeling you could ever imagine. You never realize just how lonely your life really is until you find yourself getting high all by yourself. It's just you and your conscience, and your conscience is telling you how messed up you really are. I didn't want to be alone anymore, and so I thought that by moving out to the ranch where there was always something going on, I would be a lot less lonely. My opportunity came when Andrea went out of town one weekend. I moved everything out to the ranch.

About this time, Robert Chaffee, this artist, showed up. He was an awesome painter. He moved in with us, and I had him start painting murals all around the ranch. I also had a shitload of fighters start showing up as well. Alex Ramos showed up with Jerry and "Macho" Camacho and his entire posse. The thing about Alex was that he was always singing. It was alluring having "Macho" at the ranch. I hate to admit it, but I was star struck at first. I completely stayed out of Camacho's way until one day he asked to speak to me.

At the time, Mach was staying at The Hard Rock. He had a fight coming up, and he wanted to know if he could train at the ranch. I didn't get much from having him train out there, but the ranch would get an enormous boost in prestige. I didn't just say yes, I said *hell yes!* Mach and his entire crew switched their base of operations to the ranch.

"Macho" always had a different stripper girlfriend. In fact, he kept multiple stripper girlfriends around him. They kept the ranch clean, kept his body clean, and did pretty much anything and everything else he asked of them. They were walking around naked, cooking and cleaning for him. Even for a guy like me, who had pretty much seen it all, it seemed surreal. I went out to the ranch with Jerry, and Alex, and Bones to meet "Macho." Once I arrived, it was clear what Mach wanted; he wanted to know if he could trust me. Mach poured some cocaine on my table and had me do some coke with him. I was thinking to myself . . . if he only knew. I snorted his blow, and then some more, and then some more.

"Do some more, Papi!" Mach would say. And I did. We spent the next two days doing coke and telling stories, and becoming really good friends. By day three, we all looked like zombies. All of us except for Mach. He would put on some tennis shoes, go out, and jog eight miles, and then come back and train for hours. "Macho" moved in to the ranch.

Most boxers come out to train, but "Macho" moved out there. For the next month, all kinds of celebrities, rappers, and other famous people were showing up at the ranch doing coke and partying with us. Bill had bought a pair of Excursion limousines, so we would go to the Paris Hotel and hang out. When we would go into town, everyone would want pictures of "Macho," but "Macho" wouldn't take a picture without me being in it. He would say, "Papi, Papi, get in the picture!" He even started calling me his manager. "Macho" knew everybody, and everybody knew Mach. We would get VIP treatment in every restaurant, club, and store. He even got Bones some fights. And everywhere we went, "Macho" would bend down and sniff out of his bag of cocaine, and then look up at me and ask, "Papi, Papi, am I cool?" He would have cocaine covering his nose. For the next year or so, we were pretty much inseparable.

With Mach it was partying and blow, or training and blow; it was always blow, blow, and more blow. Mach always kept at least an ounce of coke on him. He would dip four fingers into his bag of coke and sniff away, and he was so crazy that he would do it anywhere. There was no shame in him. He would walk into a casino and shout, "It's Macho Time." His bravado was contrasted by his manners and respect for the elderly.

Whenever Mach saw an old lady, he would stop and sing a song to her in Spanish while his entire entourage waited for him to finish. Mach Camacho was larger than life.

On the business side of things, life was moving forward, despite my drug-fueled partying with Camacho and his crew. I met this fireman who had invented this material called Flame Block. It was supposed to be this miracle fire retardant that was going to change the world. He had been introduced to me by this engineer who worked for the city. I had gone to get an "As Built" permit for my house, and got sold on this miracle invention. I would be the next Bill Gates, they said, if only I would put up the money to get the company going. Needless to say, I put up 60K, and both of them skipped town with my money. I ended up finding out later that the fireman guy had been on meth really bad.

Moving forward, I met this guy named Tony Lombardi, who had a partner named Johnny, who was from Denver. Tony was a car guy to the depths of his soul. He loved cars, he loved working on them, he loved selling them, he loved racing them. He was the kind of guy who could quote horsepower and torque figures for just about any car you named. He was that passionate about them. Tony and I ended up buying a car lot called Main Event Motors. Little did I know at the time that we should have named it Stripper Motors. Tony had all of these strippers coming in buying cars, and then he started giving them cars, and fixing their cars for free. We would buy all these junky cars, and he would give them away with no down payment, and we ended up losing money hand over fist. I may have made money off of one car in two years. It took me three years to get out of that business and to get those guys out of my life. It was then when I learned one of the biggest secrets about Las Vegas: everybody wanted to be somebody other than what they were. I had the car lot, the boxing management, the magazine crews, the flame retardant company, etc. . . . . I was trying to be everything but Greg, the addict. My life was devolving into complete chaos at that moment.

The chaos in my life continued, as I continued to search for my calling. I thought that I had found it when this guy named Nick showed up, and we opened up this Italian restaurant. We catered to the high rollers in Vegas by bringing in this star chef.

Opening the restaurant kept me preoccupied and away from the ranch and the cocaine-fueled parties that Camacho and his crew were constantly throwing. I felt like if I wasn't there, I could escape my urges. It didn't work. I usually just ended up snorting alone in the desert. You've never truly been lonely until you find yourself in the middle of the desert snorting cocaine on the hood of your car.

Back at the ranch, Josh kept expanding our animal inventory. We got this Clydesdale named Petty, and we got this retired racehorse named Lady, and she literally hated me. I would put a saddle on her and try to ride her, and every single time, she would take off on me like she was in a full-on race.

Usually addicts were always trying to get the horse off of their back; in this case, I had a horse trying to get the addict off of her back. Sounds crazy, but somehow, I think she knew that I was sick, that something inside of me just wasn't right. Whenever I rode her, and I could finally get her to slow down, I would trade horses. But that didn't work out any better, because I couldn't get the Clydesdale to do anything that I wanted him to. He did what *he* wanted to do.

Soon after the horses, we got two imports from Down Under. We got a kangaroo named Buster, and I added David Tua to my roster of boxers. We got Buster so that I could play with him and spar with him. Sometimes I would let all of the animals out at the same time. I would have the kangaroo, the Clydesdale, the miniature horses, and all of the other animals running around playing with each other. Except for the lions and tigers, of course. They would sit inside of their cages staring at all of the other animals while salivating and licking their chops. We were under no illusions about what would happen if one of the lions or tigers got free. One taste of blood, and old instincts would kick in. We would all be lunch.

Speaking of old instincts kicking in, I once again found myself hanging back at the ranch with Mach and the crew. We were doing everything. My pot dealer was a guy named Randy. He eventually progressed from pot, to coke, to crack, and I had progressed along with him. I found myself smoking crack cocaine once again.

Mach was still living at the ranch, and so was Bones, and so was Susie Taylor. I remember Susie training for a big fight that she had coming up, and she was in tip-top shape. We all knew Mach was coked up and that he stayed coked up, and so Susie was feeling her oats. She challenged Mach to a boxing match, and they both put on gloves and climbed into the ring. Despite Mach being all coked up, he dropped her three times in fifteen seconds. What Susie didn't know is that "Macho" fought high. Every time he stepped into a boxing ring, he was full of cocaine. Hell, he even fought better when he was high. She learned this lesson the hard way.

I left the country with Mach a short time after that. He knew that I needed to get away. We all needed to get away. I was having the bathrooms at the ranch worked on. This guy named Tino Fercola showed up, and I commissioned him to redo my bathrooms. Tino had access to materials from the Mandalay Bay, a new hotel that was being built. I wanted my master bathroom to be an exact replica of the bathrooms at the Mandalay Bay Hotel. So, we vacated the ranch and got away for a little while. Mach took me to Puerto Rico.

Mach was the king of Puerto Rico. I discovered that as soon as we landed. It literally took us an hour to get from the flight to the front door, because he had to stop and take pictures with everyone and sing songs to all the old ladies. He was the hometown hero, the boy from the projects who made good. It was Jesus, and then "Macho" Camacho, and sometimes not in that order.

So, we get to Puerto Rico, and we discovered that we've run out of coke, so "Macho" tells me to come on and let's go to this place where he knows we can score some coke, and he takes me to Le Perla.

I didn't know anything about La Perla, but let's just say it makes the worst projects in America look like a country club community. La Perla used to be an old fortress. To get to it, you drive up this long winding road, and there are these guys standing around on these walls with machine guns. And they're not police, and they're not soldiers; there was something bad going on here for sure. We pull up to the front, and this guy with a machine gun peers inside of the car and sees it's "Macho," and then gives the signal that it's okay for us to come in. So, we go into La Perla, and the first thing that you notice when you go in is that there are these guys walking around with this fishing tackle boxes. They open them up, and they are filled with every kind of drug you can imagine. You also notice that it smells like urine everywhere. It was like something out of a movie.

So "Macho" takes me deeper into La Perla. He tells me to stand with my back against the wall because if I don't, someone will walk by and stab me. "Macho" also chooses this time to tell me that I'm the only white boy that has ever been to La Perla and made it out alive. He tells me that normally, they rob the white boys, murder them, and then throw them over the walls down to the sharks. I was just glad that he used the term, "made it out alive," despite the fact that we were still in La Perla.

We made it out of La Perla after scoring our coke and headed to the press conference, and "Macho" announced to the world that he has just taken me to La Perla. I was embarrassed as heck, because everyone knows that the reason you go into La Perla is to get drugs. Anyway, we wrapped up the press conference and left. Puerto Rico was a three-day cocaine binge, and it was much needed.

The ranch was truly the sun in which many people in the boxing industry gravitated to. The article on Eddie Futch in *Esquire* magazine with the Prince Ranch logo in the background had cemented the legend of the ranch in the boxing world. I also became friends with Cameron Duncan, and this led me to co-managing a top-ranked fighter named Stephen Luevano. Stephen had been introduced to me by Cameron. George Forman's old manager, Ron Weathers, showed up as well. Ron was a total hustler. He showed up with some big guys and got me to back them, so I was now investing in some heavyweights. The newly added heavyweight boxers meant that I now had about twenty fighters. When you have that many fighters, things can get costly real fast. Managing fighters is not just about getting fights; you also have to find them houses, give them money, take care of their problems, etc. . . . It's time-consuming, hectic, and expensive. You're the counselor, the money guy, the chauffer, the manager, the marketing guy—everything. It was too much for a guy who wasn't an addict, let alone for a guy who stayed high. Still, the drama continued to come.

CHAPTER 7

The ranch became almost like a daytime soap opera. Vince , this promoter, started dating Laura Serrano and wanted to get her out of her contract and away from me. He called up Bones one day and told him that I needed to be careful and do what he said, because he knew some guys who would come to my house and rape my wife and kidnap my family. I was horrified beyond measure. Jimmy asked me what was wrong, and I told him what was going on, and just like that, Jimmy stormed away to find Vince. Word also got back to Chuck, who was one of my best friends. Turned out, we didn't have to find Vince; he found us. Vince showed up at a boxing match and upon seeing us there, tried to turn around and make for his car. Chuck raced after him and caught up to him in the parking lot. He put a grip around Vince's neck and told him that he needed to leave town and never come back. Chuck wasn't a guy that you wanted to mess

Greg Hannley

Hannah Hannley

Prince Ranch

around with. Vince disappeared and wasn't seen again for the next three years. The next time we heard anything about Vince, he had turned up at some obscure fight in Idaho.

The days of our lives' soap opera continued at the ranch. Josh had this little blonde girlfriend that he was head over heels in love with. Her name was Mai Lee, and she was an awesome female tiger handler. She also happened to be the youngest female tiger handler in the country. Well, Eric shows up, and Josh hires him as a trainer. Eric pays Josh back by banging Mai Lee. With the exception of Josh, we all knew it. One day, I saw Eric and Mai Lee kissing on the side of the cages, and I told Josh about it. Josh was my partner and my friend. He needed to know. And this set in motion a chain of events that would rock Prince Ranch, that animal training industry, and the boxing world, all at once.

My fortieth birthday arrived, and it was a spectacle that would make the Ringling Brothers Circus proud. Everyone was there. All of the boxers, the drug dealers, the strippers, the animals, everyone you could think of. I had guys on stilts, I had street mimes, pigs, tigers, lions—you name it. We had this animal trainer named Dina who had an ape fetish, letting Tarzan the Chimp play with her tits. We had all gone completely insane. I had never seen that much cocaine, pot, meth, and heroin in one place at one time. We partied like it was the end of the world. Little did I know at the time that for some of us, it would be. While for others, one world was ending, and another one was about to begin. My life was about to become unbearable.

My best friend Chuck went into the hospital for surgery on a bone spur in his shoulder. It was supposed to be a minor surgery, nothing big. I get a phone call out of the blue telling me that they messed up on his anesthesia. He flat-lined on the table during surgery, and his brain function was zero. I was at a fight with Bones in Kentucky, and I drove clear across the state to get to the hospital, and when I walked in, all of these beautiful women were there. And the crazy thing was that they were all his girlfriends, and they were all comforting one another. His parents were there as well. They were the ones who had called, and knowing what Chuck meant to me, they waited for me to get there before pulling the life support. Chuck was enormous. He had this build like a Greek statute. He was tough and strong. So strong, that it took him sixteen hours to succumb. I nose-dived into coke.

Back home at the ranch, the photographers and several other members of the press were prepping for a photo shoot with David Tua. They wanted a photo shoot of David with Jagger, the white Bengal tiger. Eric went into the tiger enclosure with Jagger to get him ready for the shoot. He had Jagger stand up on his hind legs and place his paws on his shoulders.

Jagger bit Eric in the throat and killed him instantly.

I was sitting in a bar dealing with Chuck's death when I looked up at the television screen, and see that a tiger has killed someone at the famous Prince Ranch training facility. *My ranch!*

My freaking ranch! The news said that they were still trying to get the body away from the tiger. At that time, I had no idea who had been killed. My first thoughts were on Josh.

I jumped in my car and sped to the ranch. When I got there, Mai Lee was screaming hysterically at Josh, accusing him of killing Eric. She was screaming and saying that Josh purposely didn't feed the tiger for days in order to set Eric up. She was accusing Josh of being jealous because she wanted to finally move on. That was when I realized that Josh had probably had a relationship with Mai Lee since she was young, probably as young as fourteen. I couldn't prove it, and Josh always denied it, but because of the things that she was screaming, I knew that it was obvious. I also wondered why Josh, Jagger's primary trainer, wasn't the one handling him for such an important photo shoot. Josh was my friend, and I believed him to be innocent of murder, even though I still had more questions than answers. I also wondered if my telling him about Eric and Mai Lee had led up to this, and whether I was to share some of the blame. Naturally, it was too much for me to process. I dealt with Chuck and Eric's deaths in the only way that I knew how,

I did more coke.

Eric's death brought a lot of unwanted scrutiny to the ranch, and by extension, to me. We didn't have a license to keep those kinds of animals on the ranch, so I had Josh get rid of all the dangerous ones. I also got a call from Eric's dad. I was at Chuck's funeral when he called telling me that he was going to sue me. He wanted me to fly out to Oakland and write him a check for a million dollars . . . or else. That amount continued to diminish as time progressed. Eventually, it went down to 50K and a Lincoln. The guy got nothing. He wasn't worried about losing his son; he was worried about getting something out of his death. He got absolutely nothing!

The death at the ranch was the beginning of the end of it as a premiere boxing training facility. The tiger had killed Eric during a promotional video for a big David Tua, Lennox Lewis, fight. Fighters stopped wanting to rent the house and come out there to train. They started calling it the curse of the Prince Ranch.

I started sending Andrea and Vincent out of town a lot, so that I could be free to smoke my crack in peace. This left me at home alone to binge, and that was exactly what I did. Over the course of the year I had been smoking really bad, while at the same time promising myself that I would quit. The simple truth is that you can't stop doing it, even though you know it's ruining your life. When you know that you've become a crack head, your life because horrible, Many nights, I found myself along, dirty, my fingers raw and burnt. I would often find myself in a bath robe, down on the floor, begging to find more crumbs. It was an absolutely incomprehensible demoralization. I knew deep down in my heart at the time that I needed to die; I just hoped that death would come easy.

The thing about crack is that when you did it, you always swore that it was the last time. You didn't think that it was wrong. On meth, you would get these ideas, and you would think that they were the most brilliant ideas in the world.

One night while binging, I decided to get rid of all of the animal cages at the ranch and build a baseball field. And I'm not talking about just any regular old baseball field. No, I built one with stadium lighting, and bleachers, and the whole nine yards. And next to it, I built a race car track. Never mind the fact that I didn't own any race cars. It just seemed like a brilliant idea. The even crazier thing, is that I built these things by hand, over the course of some weeks. It was my rigged up mth stadium, and I was extremely proud of it.

My birthday came around, and Andrea bought me a riding lawn mower as a birthday present. I decided to let the grass grow so that I could make this grandiose gesture toward her. In the middle of the night one evening, I wrote I love you in the grass with my new riding mower. She came out and saw it the next morning and just shook her head and walked away in disgust. That was the turning point for her, because she now knew that I was addicted to Meth.

My weird life got even weirder as time progressed. I would have nanny fights in the boxing ring, and I would have the nanny and the maid boxing each other in the boxing ring. I would make anyone who wanted to talk to me come out and play baseball while we talked. People began to suspect that I was on drugs. Either that, or they thought that I was losing my mind.

The thing about the meth world is that everyone was always selling something. People would come out to the ranch selling comic books, guns, books, paintings, furniture—hell, I even had a guy come out claiming that he was selling the original version of *The Constitution*. And the crazier thing is that they were always stealings something else while they were selling you something. It was all freaking surreal. I would buy something, realize that they stole something else, and then call them, up and buy it back from them. Also, the more I smoked, the more paranoid I became. I had cameras installed all over the ranch, and I would stay up staring into the monitors all night while shooting up or smoking meth. I smoked meth until I was on the verge of death. I could feel it coming. I knew that I had to get away.

I flew out to Washington, DC, with Mach and checked into the Watergate Hotel. The check-in was an eye-opening experience in and of itself. There was this one heavyweight champion of the world who was checking in ahead of me, and he didn't even have enough money to turn the phone on in his room. It was then when I realized that all of these ex-champs were broke. Alex had become the head of the Retired Boxers Foundation, and so, for a small time, it was headquartered at Prince Ranch. So I knew that a lot of these ex-fighters were not doing well financially, but to see these legends, and the sheer number of them, doing that bad, was eye-opening. And frightening. It scared the shit out of me, because I knew that just like them, everything that I had could be gone in an instant.

Being in D.C. took some of my stress away. Mach was always such a character to hang out with. He was the type of guy that whenever he decided something, it was time to go do it. He decided one day he needed some shoes. So we go out, and we come across this porn shop. "Macho" goes in and shoplifts a dildo from the porn shop and is walking down the sidewalk waving a dildo at everyone and shouting that it's "Macho Time." It was just typical "Macho" Camacho. He was always messing with people, having a good time and enjoying every ounce of life.

The fight we went to in D.C. was a legends fight. They had Frazier, Foreman, and all of these old fighters. "Macho" was boxing as well, and he had me work the corner. "Macho" would come back to the corner and smile and tell me to watch what he was going to do to this guy's right eye. And "Macho" would go back out into the ring and pound this guy's right eye. And then he would come back to the corner and tell us to watch what he was going to do to the guy's left eye. And then he would go and punish the guy's left eye. Once Mach was done having fun with the guy, he came back to the corner and asked if everyone was ready to go. Once we all agreed, Mach went back out and knocked the guy out instantly.

I left D.C. and flew right back to Vegas, because I had Marissa Shaw fighting on a Mike Tyson card. I was totally coked up from being in DC with Mach for three days. The cocaine, the all-night partying, and then the early flight all took its toll on me. Still, I wouldn't have missed this fight for the world. It was at this fight when I first met Iron Mike Tyson, and the legendary promoter, Don King. I got words of wisdom from both. I knew from their treatment of me that I was really on my way up in the boxing world. I had a ton of women fighters, and I was starting to be known as the King of Women's Boxing. I embraced my new title and my role, but the only problem with it was that women's boxing paid horribly.

Speaking of boxers getting paid, the most famous boxer in Mexico was coming to town. Mach and I went out and met him and took him out for a night on the town. Of course, a night on the town with Mach meant hookers, blow, and gambling. We hit the casinos with Julio César Chavez, and we were coked up to the max. Julio ended up winning at slots but didn't have his ID. Mach pretended like he didn't have his ID either. But as soon as Chavez left, Mach went and collected the money. It was typical Mach.

That cocaine-filled night left me with the strangest feeling I've ever experienced. It wasn't shame or guilt. Those were feelings that I had become used to. It felt more like a profound sadness. A sadness that reached down into the depths of my bones. It was this feeling that led me to tell Mach that I couldn't do coke like that with him anymore. I even told him that I thought that he should ease up. I told him that I didn't want to see him get killed. I don't know how Mach took my advice, but I do know that he left the ranch shortly thereafter. Again, I found myself being left alone with nothing but memories . . . and a major coke habit.

I really didn't want to shovel powder up my nose anymore. But I still needed to satisfy my high. I turned to my old friend crack, which I stated smoking a lot more. I remember going out to Joe's house, and Joe opening the door looking like a zombie from *The Walking Dead*. He had been smoking crack for a week straight. I walked inside and joined in. This time, crack wasn't going to be something I did when I wasn't doing blow or smoking weed. No, this time, crack was going to be my lover. This time, I became heavily addicted to crack cocaine.

I knew that I had a problem, because every single time I smoked crack, I swore that it would be the last time. Of course, it wouldn't be, but when you smoke crack, the guilt and shame come on soon afterward. It's like you know what you're doing is bad and wrong, and that it's destructive, but you're helpless to stop it. Your life is the slow motion train wreck that everyone is watching, and you're watching it with them, and you're completely helpless to get off. My addiction became heavy quickly, and soon, I abandoned all pretense of propriety or secrecy or dignity. I stopped having Big Al bring it to me, and I started going to Al's house and smoking it. I was the only white guy in the projects sitting on the front lawn in the projects smoking crack.

My drug binge at the ranch complimented my monotonous, business-as-usual life. The parade of characters coming by the ranch continued unabatted. That was how I met Gee.

Actually, he was introduced to me by Bones. He had been giving Bones free clothing to wear. Gee was Indian, but he was from East L.A.. He and this other character named Joey T showed up about the same time. Gee owned a clothing company and was building the brand by having boxers endorse and wear them. It was called Thug Life Clothing, and the logo was a guy holding a Mac 10, with the words 5150. Pretty quickly, Thug Life Clothing became the brand that all of the boxers were wearing. I didn't know it at the time, but Gee had a drug problem. Gee's drug problem was compounded by Joey T. Joey T had been a boxer whose manager was stealing his money, so he killed him. Joey was supposed to be in prison for life, but somehow beats his case, got out, and showed up. Actually, it came out later that Joey T was let out by the FBI to infiltrate the boxing industry and help them investigate the claim that Mexican boxers where smuggling cocaine into the country through their boxing gloves. It was never proven that this was going on, but Joey T got the benefit of the FBI's suspicion. He was one of those characters that was larger than life. Gee was scared and indebted to Joey, so he started giving Joey a bunch of clothing from the warehouse. This is the clothing that I financed. All of a sudden, Joey disappears. I go to the warehouse to check on my investment—and it's empty. This low-rent Las Vegas pimp is closing up the warehouse door, and so I ask him what's going on. I come to find out that Joey owed this guy a lot of money, and he gave him all of the clothing to clear up his debt. That was my venture into the apparel industry.

On the boxing front, the rap record label mogul named James Prince is moving into boxing in a big way. In addition to buying Floyd Mayweather's contract, he bought Bone's contract from Cameron, and since I was the co-manager with Cameron, James and I became partners. We hit it off instantly. James liked me just as much as I like him. It was also through James that I met Roy Jones Jr. When it came to boxing and business, I learned that James wasn't to be played with. It was a lesson that Floyd Mayweather Jr. had to learn the hard way. There were rumors that Floyd had tried to cut James Prince out of his contract, and Prince brought in a crew and went to the gym where Floyd was training and encouraged Floyd to do otherwise. From what I heard, Floyd cut James a check immediately, and the two ended their relationship on good terms.

I flew out to Houston to hang out with Bones at his training camp, and ended up at a party at James's house. Coincidentally, James had a thousand-acre ranch named Prince Ranch out in Houston. It was here where I met Scarface. I had no idea who he was at the time, or his place in the annuls of rap music history, I was just intrigued by his personality. In fact, I was intrigued by the whole rap culture. These guys had a lot of money, and they loved what they did. I was hooked. As soon as I got back to Vegas, I called up these local rappers that I had met and told them that I wanted to invest and become partners in the music industry. I bought into Tight With It Records, and my partners, Ju Ju, J. Bezel, Mister Feddy, and Chaos recorded our first album. It was called, "Ballers In The House." We shot the music video at the ranch. We had sixty dudes show up with low riders, and had strippers and everyone we know show up at the ranch for this rap video. Andrea awoke to find over a hundred and fifty people in the house doing a rap video. It was all insane. My partners even gave me a rap name—Big Chain.

My career as a rap mogul and a boxing manager continued to progress. Before the ranch, Andrea and I had been living on Torino Street. It was actually on Torino where I started smoking rock cocaine with Randy and Joe. Joe lived on the same block, only one lot away. There was an empty lot between our houses, and that was where we would meet up and smoke. My nanny at the time was this chick named Desire. She was also doing meth and coke unbeknownst to me. I would sneak out with Joe and smoke rock while Desire watched the kids.

Meanwhile, in the boxing world, there was this guy named Joe from Costa Rico who was a fixture in Vegas boxing. Joe was the branding guy, the guy who could get fighters paid by companies. Everybody with fighters loved Joe. He was the guy who made the checks come in. He was the good Joe. The other Joe, was Joey T, who the FBI had let out of prison to infiltrate Vegas boxing. They had put him in Top Rank. They were trying to catch Top Rank fixing fights. Rumors were also rampant about Mexican boxers bringing cocaine into fights through their boxing gloves. The FBI was trying to snag everyone at once. The cocaine, the racketeering, the conspiracy—the whole ball of wax. The bad news for me was that I was hanging out with all of the players in this big conspiracy thing. It turned out that Top Rank wasn't fixing fights, and that none of the boxers were moving cocaine. The FBI did a giant raid, but I was the only guy who they didn't talk to. For months, I was worried that the FBI was going to get me. Surely, they had seen me around all of these people, and they had to have known that I was doing cocaine with everybody.

In the midst of this time, I started hanging out at the car lot more. I also bought a couple of houses up in Big Bear, and I was continuing to get big-name fighters out to the ranch. I would hide out at the car lot, hide out at Big Bear, and do whatever I could to stay off of the radar screen. Ever seen an addict try to stay out of sight? It was virtually impossible. If I got to Jonesing bad enough, I would score from anybody and worry about the consequences after I got high. I was hooked badly. Fortunately, I had help. Big Al, my security guy, became my drug dealer. It worked out for both of us, because Big Al lived in the projects. He could pick up whatever I needed before he came to work. He even developed a system where he would hide some dope in the house, just in case I needed a hit in the middle of the night. I would call him, and he wouldn't have to drive out to the house. He would just tell me where it was hidden.

About this time in my life, my paranoia was really getting the best of me. The drugs, the FBI, Eric's death, Chuck's passing, and all of the pressures of the boxing industry . . . One of my fighters, Susie Taylor, was a heavyweight champ, and maintaining that took a lot out of a person. I knew what the drugs were doing to me, and I wanted to stop, but I couldn't stop. I took my frustrations out on everyone around me. Even Andrea. My heart was ripped into shreds when she told me that I was being mean to her, and that she understood why I was angry. She said that it was because she was getting in between me and my drugs. I was mean and cranky all of the time, and I know that I wasn't being the best father and husband. Again, my solution was to leave.

With Mach and his crew gone, I moved back out to the ranch. Soon, Al started delivering it out to the ranch again.

This door service gave me no reason to get dressed and leave the ranch. So many times I would be sitting in the bathroom in my robe with two guns, waiting for someone to break the door down. I was pretty sure that was the way it was going to end for me. I was going to die at the hands of some robber or drug dealer kicking down my door. The sad thing about it was that I felt as though I deserved to die. In my mind, I was the worst human being in the world, and I was totally worthless. I remember this one night in particular when I set up a video, and I made a video for my son Vincent. It was all of the things that a dead father wished that he could tell his son.

While Andrea was away, things took a turn for the surreal. One night, the housekeeper walked in on me and caught me with crack pipe in hand, lighting up and smoking like a crack head.

"What are you doing?" she asked.

"Nothing," I answered.

"Are you smoking crack?"

"What?" I embarrassingly hid my crack pipe behind my back. "No!"

"You're smoking crack!" she said, emphatically. "That's so ghetto."

Her response was not that I shouldn't be smoking crack because it was bad . . . but because it was ghetto. She told me that I should try this new meth instead. After that, everything changed. After that, the ranch became a hangout for meth heads. Meth is what got me off of crack. I tried to secretly do both, but I quickly found out that you couldn't do both, because doing both would make you nauseous. So it was bye-bye crack and hello meth. In adopting meth, I actually thought that I had found the solution to my crack problem.

CHAPTER 8

I was pretty deep into meth by the time Hollywood's birth came around. Andrea came back from a trip, and she was highly upset because of all these strange and crazy people around the house. There were so many things were going on. She was so upset that I had to rush her to the hospital. It was then when I learned that the difference between a baby's survival can be a matter of a week. Andrea was within three days of being within the safe period of the baby's survival. I had never been so afraid in my entire life. Time passed during the day, and they move us to the maternity ward. Their treatment was bad. The doctor coming into the room and telling us that the baby was going to come, but that she wasn't going to survive. She was a week away from her lungs being developed enough to survive. I dropped down to my knees inside of the waiting room, and I prayed. I prayed like I hadn't done since childhood. I called my sister Maureen who was a doctor and begged her to come up with some idea, some trick, some solution that the doctors in Vegas hadn't thought of. I asked my sister for a miracle, even though I knew that she wasn't the one who had the power to grant miracles. Again, I shifted my focus to The Man Upstairs.

It was one of those times when I was mad at God. I thought that He had deserted me. I was really bad on meth. A bag of meth even fell out of my pocket at the hospital, and I found myself standing on it so that the doctors wouldn't see it. I felt that it was my fault that she was going through this because of everything that I had put her through. I remember standing on that sack of meth and feeling worse than I thought it was possible for a human being to feel.

Hollywood was born, and she was born alive. The doctor handed her to me, and she was the most beautiful thing I had ever laid eyes on. Everything that was good, and right, and beautiful in the world, I was holding in my arms. I prayed as I held her in my hands, and through my tears . . . I watched her slip away.

Losing Hollywood brought the reality of a parent losing a child to me. It helped me in the work that I do today. I can relate to the pain of a parent losing a child. I never want another parent to feel the way that I felt that day, at that moment. Everything that you thought you were, everything that you thought you knew about life, everything collapses in on itself and disintegrates. You're lost. Your ability to speak, to hear, to think, to continue to move forward, it's all lost. I was a shell of a shell. Crack and meth had already hulled my life out and turned me into a figment of myself; the death of my child finished the job.

After Hollywood's passing, my brother Rob came in to town to help out, and he thought that I had gone insane. I was eating every pill that I could, smoking, drinking, and doing every drug that I could. My wife's friend brought over a tackle box of pills, and I didn't know what else to do to help her with her pain, so I just kept giving her pills. It was all completely insane, and I didn't know what else to do. The people around me were not my real friends. I wouldn't let any of my real friends come around. Everyone around me were drug relationships. They were all drug addicts. We were all in a death spiral, with the blind leading the blind. Addicts consoling an addict just meant more drugs. I knew that I had to get Andrea out of there; I knew that she didn't need to be around me or my circle. Eventually, Andrea went to Buffalo where her family was from. I was going to fly out a week later, and the plan was for me to fly out there and get clean. Always one to ruin a good plan, I was planning on taking my stash with me. This was pre-9/11, of course. I used to travel with drugs, and pipes, and needles, etc. . . . I just knew that one day I was going to be arrested at the airport in front of my family.

No one knew that I was on meth for about two years, because I hid it from everyone. Everyone just thought that I was losing my mind. My wife would ask people if they thought I was on drugs, but the people she was asking were on drugs. All of my employees, everyone at the ranch, they were all on drugs. Andrea knew that I had stopped using cocaine, and so she thought that I was clean. She didn't know what to think. Eventually, all my fighters left. I stopped showing up at fights. There would be times when I wouldn't sleep for days. And after you haven't slept for days, you go into a psychosis. And that was when things went from bad to worse.

One day I thought that I saw a bug on my face, and I started picking at it, trying to pick it out. In my mind, I was convinced that I had somehow gotten parasites while I was in Costa Rica. I would sit in the bathroom for hours, with tweezers, razors, and other sharp objects, digging and cutting chunks out of my face and arms and the rest of my skin. By the time I was finished, my bathroom would look like a murder scene. Everyone thought that I was crazy.

I finally flew out to Buffalo in an effort to get clean. I had a sales crew in Buffalo, and I was hoping that getting back on the road with the kids would help get me back on my game and out of my addiction. It didn't help. I started collecting lighters, which people thought was weird at first, but then they started giving me lighters as gifts. It had all become a little insane.

I would stay out in Buffalo for a week or two, and then I would always make an excuse to fly back to Vegas, where I would get with Anthony, my drug dealer. I would go and meet him and smoke in the garage. Funny thing about it, meth addicts always end up in a garage. No matter where you start out, you ended up in a garage.

My epic failure to get clean in Buffalo resulted in me hatching another plan. I concocted a plan to just leave and go and live on a train. I thought that my life would be fine if I could just go and live on a train. I went to the Hyatt Regency, and I was planning on living on a train. Andrea found me in the hotel, and she brought me back to Buffalo. She knew, even without saying it. But I knew that she knew. We grabbed the kids and headed for Florida. I thought that I could clean up in Florida. I always thought that if I could find a new place, I could get clean. I kept telling myself that all I needed was a new start. But relocation therapy never works. Never has, never will. We flew out to Florida, and once I ran out of dope,

I would make an excuse and fly back to Vegas. I would keep Andrea out of town and occupied as much as I could. I would fly out to Vegas, and again, I would stay up for days getting high, and sure enough, the parasite would come back, and I would start cutting out chunks of my face.

I eventually found out that my brother-in-law was on meth. He found out because we were barbecuing once and he caught me with a box cutter cutting a chunk of meat out of my leg, thinking that I was cutting out a parasite. He found me sitting in a chair surrounded by a pool of blood. I would cut out chunks of flesh and pull out veins, thinking it was the parasite's hair. He recognized the symptoms. He and I started getting high together all of the time after that. I would make excuses to go out and visit him, and we would always end up in the garage getting high.

The parasite things started getting really bad. I was cutting out pieces of my face. The way that I chose to deal with it was to go out and buy a Maserati and a Prince CD. I remembered 1982 as being the happiest time in my life. My boss had this red Maserati, and we were always riding around listening to Prince. So, I found the exact same car on eBay and bought it and bought a Prince CD. I was thinking that I could re-create those times, and if I did it just right, then all of my problems would just go away.

They didn't.

I went to the parasitic institute in order to get rid of the parasites. They couldn't help me. They said that I didn't have any parasites, and that I needed to stop cutting off chunks of flesh. I thought that they were full of shit, because I knew for a fact that I had parasites. And since they couldn't help me, and since the parasites were going to eat me from the inside out, I did what I figured was the next best thing. I drove out to Malibu with the nanny, and we stayed up for five days smoking meth and pretending like it was the end of the world.

I knew that I was going to die. I had planned to live it up, and run up my American Express card, and die. Andrea would get a million dollars from my insurance policy, and the kids would get a good dad, and everyone would be all right.

It was my son's sixth birthday, and I knew that I was going to die that day. I started calling people up and saying good-bye, telling people that I was going to die. I thought that the parasite and the worms inside of my body were going to eat up my heart. Everyone was getting worried. They thought that I was going to kill myself. Even the meth addicts around me were getting worried.

Bones flew out to Malibu to get mea and drive me back to Vegas to Doctor Voy's office to see if he could help me. Dr. Voy was one of the most famous doctors in boxing. He let me cut out some pieces of my skin and show him some of the worms. He didn't know what to do with me, so he sent me over to another doctor, and he wrote a note for me to give to the other doctor. I read the note that he sent with me. I read,

"This is my friend, treat him with respect."

After reading Dr. Voy's note, I knew then that I was imagining things. The other doctor knew that I was on meth. He called Dr. Voy and the two of them had a long private conversation about me. Once they were done, he sent me back over to Dr. Voy's office. Doctor Voy told me that he had good news and bad news for me. First, he told me that I wasn't going to die, but that I had parasitic psychosis. He had me count the days since I last slept. It had been eleven days. I didn't know what to do or what to say. I had told everyone that I was going to die. I asked him what I was going to tell everyone. He said to tell everyone that he cured me. He told me to get some sleep and to come back and see him. But I never went back. I couldn't face him.

I did, however, go back to meth. I was an addict. My solution to the problem was to make sure that I never stayed up for more than two days. That may have solved the psychosis, but it didn't solve my other problems. I was spending up the money from my company.

I had everyone treating me like I was insane, and to top it off, Andrea was pregnant again. My meth-inspired solution was to demolish my kitchen in the middle of the night. I thought that I could change my house, that it would start to change my life. I thought that remodeling my home would also remodel my life. I was wrong. But that was the meth talking to me. It would just keep my mind busy coming up with all of these ideas to draw attention away from the real problem: my addiction.

The meth voices in my head would inspire me to get up at night or early in the morning and go to Home Depot with my meth girls and do ridiculous things like buy up all of the plants and flowers and have pallets of sod delivered so that I could redo my lawn. There was the time when I got the meth-inspired idea to break the record for flying the highest kite in the world, so me and my meth girls went and bought up all of the kite string at every Walmart and Target in Vegas. People would come by and see all of this kite string on the ground and ask what the hell I was doing, and I would tell them that I was going to break the world record, like it was all something rational. There was also the time when I wanted a million Christmas lights on my home, so me and my meth girls went to every Walmart and Target and bought up all of the Christmas lights, blow up decorations, and extension cords. My meth girls, as I call them, were all my smoking buddies. They were all aspiring actresses, in beauty school, or massage therapy school, or something of that nature. They were all just as sick as I was. Worst of all, my addiction was beginning to take a heavy toll on my marriage.

Andrea started feeling the same way she felt when she lost Hollywood. We went to the hospital, and I already knew what was going to happen. This time, I didn't call anyone, I didn't pray to God, we just went through it again. I thought that I couldn't feel lower. And again, I blamed it on myself. I chewed pills and did drugs. I went out into the desert, climbed out of my car, took off all of my clothes, and I sat on the hood of my car and did meth until I couldn't see. I could hear the coyotes in the distance, howling. I stood on the hood of my car, and I howled back at them. I wanted them to come and find me. I didn't want anyone to find my worthless body. I would be okay if the coyotes devoured it. I stayed in the desert all night getting high on meth, daring the coyotes, the bobcats—anything—to come and help me end the pain.

I woke up the next morning on the hood of my car. The desert sun had already started baking me. I decided to go home. The home that I decided to go to wasn't the one in Vegas, nor the ranch outside of Vegas, but home. I felt that I could go home and clean up. I flew to my mom's house in Arizona.

I flew home, and I told my mom how horrible Andrea was, and I thought she was on my side. My mom's reply, however, was that she didn't know why Andrea stayed with me. Her advice to Andrea would be to leave me right away. She knew I was on drugs. Everyone knew that I was on drugs. No matter how much I thought I was hiding it, they all knew.

My run to Arizona just happened to be on Mother's Day. Upon finding out where I was, Andrea decided to fly out, and she was angry the whole time she was there. For the life of me, I couldn't figure out why. Everything was her fault. I had convinced myself that it was all her fault. Eventually, she left and flew back home to Vegas.

I knew that I had to go back to Vegas and make things right with Andrea. I knew that I should've taken the first flight out, because Jimmy was throwing me a birthday party back in Vegas as well. This would have been the perfect opportunity to make up with Andrea. She couldn't be mad at me on my birthday, could she? Anyway, I spent the morning smoking meth and celebrating my birthday alone. I ended up missing every plane and finally catching the last plane and made it over to the house just in time to find out that everyone had left when they found I wasn't going to make it. And just my luck, my friend Billy had a heart attack while cooking dinner for me.

I continued to use heavily over the next couple of months. On the meth circuit, I met this black guy who was also a meth user. He told me that he was using bleach to bleach his skin, and that if I bathed in bleach, I could get rid of the parasites. So I did it and had bleach burns over my entire body. I lied and told everyone that it was from a cream that I bought in Mexico.

It was about this time when Jimmy started getting sick, and so I went to stay with him and take care of him. I don't think I was much help to him, as I ended up on his couch getting high all of the time. This is when I discovered OxyContin. I used it, but it gave me a splitting headache. Thank God for that; otherwise, it would have been another drug on my long list of abuse. I stuck with good old reliable meth.

By this time, it was pretty much a known fact that I was using, and using bad. I just stopped lying about using and came out into the open and told people that I was an addict. Once you state that, you've pretty much given up, and you're pretty much in your death spiral. Word got back to Ken up in Seattle. Ken, who was going through recovery himself, introduced me to this guy named Mark, who pretty much invented disco back in the '70s. Ken also told Mark that I was using. Mark was friends with the guy who owned the recovery center that I would eventually go to, and he knew a lot about recovery. Never one to mince words, Mark told Ken straight out that if I didn't get treatment, I would be dead in a month. He said that I would either overdose or kill myself. The crazy thing about it, was that when Ken insinuated that I was going to kill myself, I was furious. Little did I know that two weeks later, I was going be making plans to drive up to Mt. Charlestown and shoot myself. Two weeks after that, I was sitting in the garage at the ranch with a .45 pointed at my chest, begging Andrea to let me go, because I didn't want to kill myself at the ranch. Some how she figured out what I was planning to do, and she intervened. She wouldn't leave me alone, and she eventually talked me out of the car and into the house. Within the period of a year, I had lost two babies, I had mismanaged the company to near bankruptcy, and I had destroyed my skin.

Ken would never leave me alone. He had flown into town and was staying at Bill's place while he got the company situated again. I overspent by 600K and almost ruined thirty years of hard work in the magazine industry. Ken kept trying to do interventions with me, and he was always around talking about peeling back an onion. I hated him. I thought that he was going to ruin me and take away my company. One day, I found myself sitting in my Suburban, with my dad's .45, thinking that I was going to have to drive over to Bill's house and shoot Ken. Fortunately, one of my crew managers named Chris drove up and asked me what I was doing. When I told Chris that I was going to drive over to Bill's house and shoot Ken, Chris told me to give him the guns. He took the gun out of my hand and told me to call Desire and go and get a massage, and that he would go over to Bill's house and if he thought Ken needed to be shot, then he would shoot him. Being high at the time, I thought it was a great idea. I called Desiree and went to get a massage.

About this time, Bones got beat up really bad by Tony Ayala. The doctor wrote Bones a prescription for Valium, and naturally, I took it. It made me feel a little better. I was on Vicodin, Soma, Valium, crack, and vodka at this time in my life. I had a friend named Sue Wiggins, who was working with Tony Robbins this time. Sue knew that I was sick. She had me fly out to Dallas, which I did, and the next thing I knew, I was at Tony Robbins' walking on fire. I spent time out there getting well, and it seemed like things were getting themselves in order. I flew back home renewed, and within a couple of weeks . . . I was back on drugs. No matter what I tried, I couldn't seem to escape it. Even up at my home in Big Bear, places that were supposed to be my respite from drugs, I found myself using. I was definitely in my death spiral.

Over the next couple of months, Ken kept coming down from Seattle, trying to get me help. His last resort was to cut me off from all money. He had me resign from the board of directors, which I didn't realize meant that the board could cut me off from any money. So he had them cut me off, and I had to convince the board that I would go for an evaluation at a treatment center. Once the center said that I didn't have a problem, the board would turn my money back on. The other condition was that the board would give me all of my power back, and Ken would be fired.

Within a week, I went and met the crew in La Jolla, where we were getting ready to go down to Ensenada for vacation. Bill and Ken wanted me to meet with Mark again, since he had a connection at a treatment center that could get me in. I went to the treatment center, and found myself sitting on a bench next to a guy who asked me what I was in for. I told him that I was just here to get an evaluation so that I could get my company back. He told me that he was on crack and that he couldn't get off of crack. He told me how his life had spun out of control, how he had lost his wife, his kids, the rest of his family. Within five minutes of talking to this guy, I knew that I wanted to stay. I now felt that instead of trying to talk my way out, I wanted I wanted to talk my way in. This was Dec. 15, 2003.

During the initial meeting at the rehab, the case manager asked me when I wanted to come in. I told him that I had Christmas, and a boxer negotiating a Miller Light contract, and the trip to Ensenada coming up. I had a thousand reasons why I should check in after Christmas. His answer to me was, "Now. How about now?"

I thought about it deeply for some moments. I really wasn't ready to check in that day, I was thinking more along the lines of January 3rd. We came to an agreement that the 15th of December would be good. That would give me enough time to wrap up my immediate concerns. They also agreed to let me go home for Christmas with a sober companion. At the time, Andrea was pregnant again. I felt like I didn't want to stay home, because I really wanted her to have this baby. I could be the cause of her losing another child. Besides, I was tired, really, really tired. I just wanted to rest. I figured that thirty days would be good enough for me to rest, and it would give Andrea time to rest and carry the baby into a period where it would be able to survive. I agreed to the check-in date, and spent the next couple of days getting as high as humanly possible. I didn't know much about treatment then, and I didn't know that you could come in high or drunk, so I spent two days sobering up before I went in.

CHAPTER 9

I walked in to wrap up, which is where people talk about what they did that day, and I told them why I was there. Andrea was pregnant again, and I wanted to give her some peace, because we had lost the last two babies. I learned that the treatment center that I was at was a really high-profile treatment center with a lot of famous people. I was the low guy on the totem pole. I remember sitting on the bench that first night thinking that I couldn't believe that this had happened to me. I couldn't believe that I was sitting in a drug treatment center. The next morning came and everyone was going to the gym to work out and play basketball, but I couldn't go because my blood pressure was 200 over 100. Usually, I would have been the first guy in the car, but I had to stay at the center. I'm glad that I did, because I got to have a really good conversation with a famous actor, and my eyes were opened to a lot of things. First off, I didn't realize how much people paid to get treatment, and that they relapsed and came back and paid that crazy amount of money again. It was an insane circle.

Prior to entering drug treatment, I had been following Tony Robbins around, trying to fix things that were wrong. What I learned from Tony was that I was a really resentful guy, and that I hated everyone around me that didn't act the way I thought they should act, even without me telling them. I learned in one of the groups at the center that there was no room in my heart for healing, and that if I carried around all of that resentment, I would never be able to fully heal. It was then when I realized that I was in for a rough patch for the next six months.

While I was there, this really famous actor came in, and we sat with on that bench the first night he was there. The guy sang an entire New York musical for me while we sat there. It was my second night, his first, and I think that we were both worried about what sleep would bring. I could tell that he was nervous, scared, uncertain, and me just being there to listen was therapeutic for both of us. Life had thrown both of us one helluva curve ball. We worked our way through rehab together, and we're still really good friends to this day. I often think back to that moment, to those guys who were there when I first got there. Out of our original group of twelve, more of them are dead than alive.

During my stay at the rehab, I found myself calling my office almost daily. I was sure that Ken was stealing my company, and that he was purposely trying to ruin my world. I would tell Debbie the receptionist that I had to leave, and she would calm me down and get me to go to another group. When she wasn't around, Harry, this sixty-five-year-old addict who loved jazz, would calm me down and get me to stay. We called Harry, "Cool Breeze." He had this calming, deep, baritone voice that was mellow and soothing. He would have had a heck of a jazz career if addiction hadn't gotten to him early in life. That was always how it was, wasn't it? We all had plans, goals, talent, ambition—and then life always found a way to get in the way.

I would take my recovery one meeting at a time. One meeting at a time led to one day at a time. There were times when I had to take it one second at a time, and allow the seconds to build up to minutes, and the minutes to roll into hours. I learned that after ten days of being in recovery, people would go to sober living. At that time, it cost $23,000 for drug treatment. Outpatient cost $6,500. It was always more than I could afford, let alone more than I actually had. Fortunately, I had one more swipe on my American Express Card, and I used it to pay for two weeks of sober living. It was the best purchase that I had ever made.

While in rehab, I wrote this scathing letter about Ken and how much I hated him. To me, everything was Ken's fault. Me being in recovery, me having to go to rehab, losing control of my company, being cut off from my money—it was all Ken's fault as far as I was concerned. I didn't see Ken as helping me.

I didn't understand that Ken was being a better friend to me than all of the people around me who allowed me to use freely. I viewed my meth girls as friends and Ken as the enemy. It would take some time for me to heal enough to understand. But I can say that the letter I wrote never got to Ken. I left the letter there.

When my time was coming up to end my stay in the sober living community, I had no idea what I was going to do.

Debbie told me to pray on it. I was just beginning to reconnect with God again. I had gone into rehab really angry at God. Everything that I had asked for, I was never given. I thought of God as being someone who played really cruel tricks on me.

I was about twenty days sober when Andrea came for a visit one weekend. We went out and drove around Malibu. I wanted to show her a beautiful sunset, and we got completely lost. We drove past the elementary school, the high school, and we drove down this one-way street into this cul-de-sac. Every house on the street was adorable. The views were incredible, and everything seemed so peaceful, so Americana. The neighborhood looked like it belonged in a television commercial. Andrea looked at me and said that if there was any place in the world she wanted to live, it was on that street. I agreed.

Back at the rehab, Debbie told me to ask God for inspiration. I knew that I couldn't go back to Vegas because I knew that I would die there. The same people, the same environment, the same everything, I would be dead in a month. I had come to a crossroad. I know that if I took a left on my road, I would head to Vegas, a right would lead toward Malibu. I knew what direction I wanted to go in, but I knew what I could afford. Malibu wasn't a viable option.

Susie, one of my old boxers, came to visit, and we went out together. While out, I ran across a small newspaper with an ad that said, "We rent houses." I called the listed number, and this lady answered the phone. She asked me to describe the house that I wanted. I told her that I wanted four bedrooms, with an ocean view, for about $5,000 a month. She said that she might have something.

I met with the lady at Morning View Road and Pacific Coast Highway, and I followed her. She led me past the elementary school and the high school, back to the very same neighborhood where Andrea said that she wanted to live. Ecstatic beyond control, I called Andrea and told her that this real estate lady was taking me to that neighborhood we fell in love with. Andrea, being the practical one, asked why. We didn't have any money because I had blown everything. I knew that Andrea loved the neighborhood, and I knew that us getting lost and finding this place couldn't have been an accident. I told the real estate agent that I didn't even need to see the house, because I knew that I was supposed to live there.

My restored faith in God had not resulted in a restoration of my bank account, however. I pretended to fumble around in my wallet, and eventually, I told the agent that I had forgotten my checkbook. I convinced her that I was going to get the house, and begged her to not show the house to anyone else. I signed a contract on the house standing in the driveway.

I took all of my friends from the center and showed them this house that I was going to live in. It was a fantastic weekend, but Monday-morning reality set in, and I was left wondering how I was going to pay for this house. I prayed hard.

I got a phone call from Mike Moga from Tucson later that day. The agent had told me that the cost to move in to the house was $15,600. During our call, Mike told me that he got this refund from this Rolls-Royce that we had put a deposit on, because we had been in the classic car business years ago. I never thought that I would hear from Mike again. I asked Mike how much the refund was for, and he told me $15,000. I gave Mike my bank info, and he put the money in the bank.

The crazy part was that since the month had started, the total amount I had to pay was prorated, which meant I only had to pay $14,900. After that, it was pretty obvious to me that God had never left me. He had always been there. I called Andrea to tell her what happened and that we got this house, and that we could now move to Malibu. Andrea was practical. She asked how I could have spent all the money on that house when that was all the money we had. My answer was for her not to worry, because God wanted us to have this house.

I flew back to Vegas so Andrea could have the baby, and I felt good. For the first time in a long time, I felt as though my future was bright, and that God and I were on good terms again. This newfound feeling didn't last very long, though. The third day that I was there, Andrea said she wasn't feeling well.

I knew what was happening.

I drove the kids to school, and then took Andrea to the hospital. The doctors told us that she was going to lose the baby, and I stayed there with her until she lost it. Afterwards, I picked the kids up from school, went back to the hospital and picked Andrea up, and drove them home. The drive home was surreal. I felt like I was living in a bad nightmare, everything seemed so mechanical to me, like I was just going through the motions of life, and not actually living. The pain inside was indescribable. It was déjà vu all over again, and It was like I was in a horrible fog. I dropped them all off at home, and then I went to the grocery store, and the first thing you see when you walk into a grocery store in Vegas is the liquor. I knew that it would be so easy to pick up that bottle and start drinking again. I was upset with God again. This wasn't supposed to be the deal. And like a dumb ass, I wanted to use again, I wanted to destroy my life, as if that would somehow get back at God. Fortunately, God didn't see things that way.

A friend called and asked how I was doing, and I told him what happened. His advice was to stay strong. He reminded me of what I had gone through, and how much Andrea and the kids needed me. I went home and told Andrea that I couldn't stay in that house another moment. I didn't have the money to move, but I prayed about it again. The next morning, the phone rang. It was an old friend who called and said that she was doing well, and that she could afford to pay me back the money she had borrowed. I didn't even remember how much it was. Turned out it was $3,500. It was enough to move. I loaded up my family, and we moved to Malibu. Still, I had no idea how I was going to pay rent.

Ken still wouldn't give me any money; he was afraid that I was going to go back to using drugs. This just made me even more furious at Ken. I was out of rehab, I was clean, and I needed access to my money. Ken wasn't buying it.

Once we arrived in Malibu, I got a call from the mortgage company who did my refinance on the ranch. They had sent me a check to the ranch, but it came back. They wanted to know what I wanted them to do with the check. It was for $27,000. I was able to pay my rent for several months, and pay my credit cards. Somehow, someway, things like this happened consistently. Every month, something happened that would allow me to pay my rent.

I made some friends around Malibu, and I was still managing some fighters in Vegas. I still didn't know what to with myself. I was introduced to Ash Adams, who was making a boxing movie. I ended up becoming partners on this movie called *The Distance*.

Ash took me under his wing, and we would go out, go shopping, go eat on the town. Ash was also the one who introduced me to my friend and sponsor, Scotty Brown. Many people don't realize when you come out of recovery, you really have no social skills. You've been living around addicts for so long, and you've been distant from functional society for so long that you really don't know how to act in social situations.

Addicts have no filter and no social graces. I met Scotty at the Malibu film festival. He was this big bald guy from Chicago.

Scotty and I became friends really quick. He was always invited to cool parties, and he would take me along with him. I would watch how Scotty interacted with people, and that was what taught me how to be a human being again. It was from Scotty that I got my social courage.

Being able to hang out with others is something that others take for granted. I remember one time when one of the neighbors was having a barbecue, and I really and truly didn't know how to interact with people. I went and stayed for fifteen minutes. I guess the neighbor noticed that I left kinda early, so he invited me back to another barbecue where it would just be his family. To top it off, Andrea's chiropractor invited us to a barbecue that he was throwing as well. The idea of having to repeat the experience two more times had me so freaked out, that I actually had to go to meet up with my friend and sponsor Scotty Brown to calm my nerves.

About this time, my friend Scotty had a gotten a green light for a show called, *Million Dollar Listing*. Scotty asked me to be on the show, supposedly buying this massive, million-dollar mansion. As for my real financial situation, well, it wasn't too rosy. I still didn't have any money, so Bones brought over this box of jewelry and let me take it and get a loan against it.

I met Alex Draghici who was at this company called 111 Productions. Alex was one of the producers on this movie called *The Distance*. Alex and Floyd gave me an office at 111 Productions, and I set up a sales team. All of a sudden, I was now in the advertising business. I reached out to an old friend of mine named Ron, from Vegas. Ron managed to get me another loan using my ranch as collateral for about $200,000. Unfortunatrely, Ron immediately absconded with $60K of it, which left me with $140,000. I spent $100K of it at 111, and then 111 folded. Just like that, I was out of the production business.

I went back to Vegas to take care of things, and as usual, the first thing that I did when I got back into town was go see Anthony. It was always the first thing I would do whenever I hit Vegas. I called my sponsor and told him that I was going to go and visit Anthony, and, of course, my sponsor asked if I thought that was a good idea. Old habits die hard, but I resisted the urge to go and see Anthony. It was one of the hardest moments I had in my recovery journey.

Bad ideas kept popping up. On the way to the ranch, I decided that I was going to stop and see Leslie, another meth dealer, who operated out of a bike shop. I had run over my son Vincent's bike and was thinking that I would stop in and pick him up another one. Again, my sponsor asked if I thought that would be a good idea. Going to get a stolen bike from a meth dealer was definitely not a good idea. I called my sponsor constantly while I was in Vegas. Every hotel, every corner, every place I went and looked at was a reminder. Every street, every turn, every familiar person that I saw was a trigger. I knew that I needed to hurry up and get out of Vegas.

About this time, there was this group called the Focus Group that was buying up all of the properties around the ranch. They contacted me and offered me half a million dollars for the ranch. Naturally, I turned it down. That ranch was worth more than that. Back in California, Scotty took me out to this place called the Doom Room. There was nothing to do there but drink. He and I talked about it and thought how cool it would be to have a place to go to for sober people. We would call it the SoBar, which was short for Sober Bar. The dilemma for people in recovery was that after the meetings were over and Starbucks was closed, there was absolutely nothing to do.

One day, Scotty took me over to this little weird barbershop, and we see this overgrown, dirty parking lot. This shitty little duplex, with this older guy name Gene, who was in the garage. The entire place smelled like raw sewage. Scotty tried to get me to see something that wasn't there, and I really wasn't interested. I had something else in mind.

I changed the ranch to a sober-living facility. So now the ranch was going to be the Prince Ranch Sober Living Facility. I flew my cook's friend out to the ranch to get sober, and unbeknownst to me, the guy relapsed and was doing drugs and having hookers up in the ranch. It was crazy.

I get another call from Focus Group, and this time they offer me $900,000. The ranch was in the middle of the other properties that they had already bought. I knew that they were going to knock it down, and I also knew that the ranch was smack-dab in the middle of their other properties and that they needed it. I was that last holdout, and they were desperate. I countered their $900K offer with a $2.8 million asking, with $100K nonrefundable earnest money, with a sixty-day limit, and a stipulation that I would have one year to remove any of my fixtures from it, because I knew that they were going to tear it down. It was an absolutely ridiculous counter, and I knew that there was no way that they would go for that. As soon as the offer was faxed, I received an acceptance on that offer with an agreement to all terms. I was shocked.

Once the realization set in that I had accidentally sold my ranch, I went and asked my friend Ronnie, who was a retired real estate agent, if I had to go through with it. Ronnie's answer was yes, that I had to sell it. So now, it was a countdown. Within sixty days, the Focus Group put the money in my account, and I knew that I had really sold it.

By now I had become friends with yet another Jimmy. This Jimmy was guy from Boston who had twenty four years sober, and who had fallen on hard times. I let him live on the sofa in my garage. I knew that I needed to go to the ranch and collect my belongings and to sell the furniture, but I didn't want to go alone. I recruited Jimmy to go get up off of the sofa and go with me and be my sober companion. I headed out to the ranch with Jimmy, and on the way he tells me that he's going to drink. So, instead of Jimmy taking care of me and being my sober companion, I ended up taking care of him. In the end, it ended up helping me out even more, because I was so caught up in saving Jimmy, that I didn't think of using myself.

As far as the ranch was concerned, the easiest thing that I could have done would have been to just donate everything, and get a huge tax write-off. I called around and was trying to get people to come out and take things, and no one wanted to take anything. Susie came out to help, and she convinced me to have an estate sale. Trust me, the worst thing you could ever do is to have an estate sale when you're still alive. I had no choice. So, I opened up my door to sixty rats. People who wanted to give me fifty cents for items priced a dollar. It made me depressed.

I always thought that the ranch was where my life was supposed to be. And watching it be carted away, piece by piece, by cheap vultures, was like watching your own carcass being eaten. I was going to make a million dollars on the sale of my ranch, but felt like it wasn't worth it. To make matters worse, I got a call from Gary, my tax attorney, who informed me that I was going to end up owing more than a million dollars in taxes on the sale of my ranch. I would owe more than what I was getting, unless I did what was known as a 1031 exchange. I was *really* depressed.

Again, I turned to The Man Upstairs, and I asked God what the deal was. The answer came almost immediately afterward. Scotty called me and told me that the property that I hated didn't sell. He said that if I moved on it right then, I could get it. I asked how much they wanted to sell it for, and he told me 2.8 million, the exact amount that I needed for the 1031 exchange. Once again, God had answered my prayers.

Everything changed at the estate sale. I started giving things away at the estate sale. I gave this one young couple who needed a twin bed enough furniture to fill several rooms. People who needed things started coming. A woman whose husband was killed in Iraq needed furniture, and I gave her enough furniture for an entire apartment. At the end of the estate sale, a gentleman named Tom Holmes showed up from Aardvark Construction out of Utah. He made up a story about he and his crew needing a place, because the place where they were saying was horrible. He said that their equipment kept getting broken into, and his crew was all staying in separate locations. He would pay $7,500 a month cash if I would let him stay at the ranch. I told him that they had one year to live there. Tom said that his partner wanted to see the place, but no one could be there when his partner came. Which I thought was super weird. Still, I explained that the house was sold, and that they could live there, but couldn't do anything to the house. Tom promised that they wouldn't. Unbeknownst to me, I had just rented out this house to the most wanted man in America— the polygamist Warren Jeffs and his family.

About a month and a half later, I had a fight scheduled in Nogales. My plan was to fly out and see my mom first, but I got a phone call from the building department in Vegas, informing me that I needed a permit for all of the construction going on at the ranch. Instead of flying out to Arizona I ended up flying out to Vegas to see what was going on. When I arrived at the ranch, it was clear that the entire interior of the ranch had been gutted, and there was a six-foot high pile of debris sitting outside of the ranch. I walked in to what used to be my office, and all I saw was racks and racks of bags of flour, sugar, and canned food. There was enough to feed several hundred people for a long, *long* time. My gym had been converted into a school with desks and chalkboards, and where the bathroom used to be, there was now a massive commercial laundry. The other office was now a huge commercial kitchen. In what used to be the dining room, there were now two huge tables with enough seating to seat sixty people. On an entire side of one of the tables was nothing but high chairs. In the bedroom, there were forty bunk beds.

Forty!

The stairs that used to lead to the top suite now led to nowhere. They had walled the stairs. The second living room had been converted into a chapel. The more I explored my former home, the more freaked out I was starting to become. They had even taken one room and filled it up with sewing machines, and another room was full of canning machines. Upstairs, what used to be two huge bedrooms had now been converted into several bedrooms. There were several cribs, and even a damn birthing room. I asked Tom Holmes how many people were living there, and he said about a hundred and seventy-five. I then asked where they were. He said he sent them all out to lunch. In reality, they were all hiding. I told Tom that they needed building inspections or the city was going to start shutting down the utilities and start fining them $500 a day.

Things went from weird to weirder when Tom informed me that they were not using city utilities anymore. I told him that the city was going to have to come and inspect, and Tom's answer was that they couldn't allow that. It was then when I thought about the fencing, the makeshift towers, and the berm and debris. Waco was the foremost thought on my mind. It wasn't until I remembered that Warren Jeffs had just been captured down the street from the ranch, that I put two and two together and realized that I was sitting in hid polygamy compound. I got the hell away from the ranch as quickly as I could.

I flew to Tucson where I had dinner with my mom and my two brothers, and I told them what happened. We were all a little freaked out about the entire situation, but there was nothing that I could really do about it. I wasn't sure if there was anything that I wanted to do about it. I figured that the legal authorities would handle things in due time.

I went to the fight in Nogales, and then flew back to Malibu the next day. Back in Malibu, I went to the guy who owned the complex and asked if I could start cleaning up the place. It was going to be my place as soon as we went through closing, but I was anxious to get a jump on things. I went out to the place with chain saws and started cleaning up, cutting away all of the overgrowth. While cleaning and clearing, I soon discovered that we could actually see the ocean from the property. I rented the apartment in the complex and moved the guy living in my garage into the apartment. He would be onsite, cleaning and clearing and watching my investment until all of the paperwork went through and I officially took ownership.

The bank assured me that they had the loan for the ranch, and that they would transfer the loan over to the duplex. Unfortunately, I had to fly back out to the ranch to do the loan inspection with the bank. The bank appraiser and I went to tour the house, and when we opened up the door to this one room, on the wall was this huge picture of Warren Jeffs.

The loan fell apart on the new property, so I had to find an alternate source of financing. I went with these hard money lenders out of New York called Madison Realty Capitol. They wanted six months' interest up front, which amounted to $200,000, which I didn't have. Fortunately, my next-door neighborhood, Ron, said that he knew somebody who could do the loan. It turned out to be the mob.

Meyer Lansky's brother told me that for $25,000, he could get me the loan. Meyer Lansky had been one of the most notorious and long lived mafia personas in the history of the country. His brother had come into town with his home-shopping girlfriend on other business. I had no other choice, so I wrote him a check for $25,000, and got ripped off for it. Even worse than losing the money, the clock was still ticking on the deadline to change over the loan. Uncle Sam was definitely licking his chops for his million-dollar tax check for the sale of the ranch.

I didn't know it at the time, but the guy who I had let stay on my couch was doing good, and he had told his dad that he was doing good. So, the dad sent me $50,000, and told me that it was the least he could do for me saving his son's life. To top it off, two different neighbors gave me ten grand apiece, saying that they really wanted him to get SOBA going. I really had a feeling that things were going to work out. So, on the final day of the sale of the ranch, I get a call from the title company saying that they couldn't close the loan because the building had a red tag from the city.

I called the lady from the building department and told her that the new owners were going to knock down the house, and that I had accidentally rented the house to Warren Jeff's polygamy family. I also explained to her that if the loan didn't close, I would have to move back to Vegas into that ranch. I explained to her that I was a recovering drug addict, and that if I moved back to Vegas, I was going to die. The lady said that she had never done this in the twenty years that she had worked in the building department, but she understood what I was going through. Her son was an addict. She told me to tell the title company to try to close the loan again. She pulled the red tag, the title company closed the loan, and then she put it back on. I breathed a huge sigh of relief. The polygamist was no longer my problem.

A couple of months later, when the city was running them out of town, Tom Holmes called me wanting his security deposit back. I told him that he was crazy. He had completely gutted and destroyed the ranch. The next time I saw that group, they were on the news in Texas—for doing the exact same thing in Texas.

CHAPTER 10

‌⟢⟜

Back in Malibu, Gene, the owner of the property that I was trying to buy, said that he wasn't going to extend the escrow any longer. I was still $180,000 short. Just when I was about to give up, the phone rang, and it was the title company telling me to come down and sign. I told them that I was still $180,000 short. They told me not to worry about it. The two real estate agents had waived their commissions, and the owner lowered the price by $60,000. I got the place. What I hadn't realized in my complete joy and elation was that I actually closed on December 15th, the anniversary of my sobriety date.

I now owned the building, but the problem was that I inherited tenants along with the property. All of my units were occupied. I had four different families living on property, and I didn't want to kick anyone out. I decided to wait them out.

One by one, they left. All except one. The guy that remained was a preacher. I went to him one day, and I told him that I wished that I could have that last apartment. To my surprise, he said that God came to him in a dream and told him that he should move. He moved the next day.

The original idea for SOBA was that it was to be a hangout place for people who were sober. What it turned out to be was the first independent sober living place in Malibu. We got the people that no one else wanted. We were the last stop on the line for many people. I wanted to do more to help.

I learned a few key words about recovery and therapy and treatment. I went to a class at LMU called Choice Theory in Addiction Recovery that was taught by Dr. Glaser. What really woke me in that class was that he was telling me that with your kids, if you bribe them or coerce them, your relationship gets further away. If you get into a situation where you're trying to guide them in a new direction, it works. I decided to apply this theory to SOBA.

At SOBA, we started saying that we were a social model recovery community with an emphasis on choice theory. People liked that idea, or at least they liked all of the fancy terminology. Shortly after emphasizing Choice Theory, I became a member of the board of directors of the Los Angeles Sober Living Coalition.

Back at the new facility, all of this newfound attention meant that we had to actually look the part. In the morning, we got up and painted and worked, went to a noon meeting at Serra Retreat, then we'd come home and paint and work, and then barbecue and go to the night meeting. Before we realized it, we'd stayed sober for another day. In the midst of all this, the polygamist moved out, so we went to the ranch and took out all of the fixtures, decks, and lights and brought them back to sober living and reinstalled them. We even replanted all of the plants from the ranch at the duplex. We also started having really good success with people staying sober.

I still owned a trailer park in Hemet, California, so if someone fell off, I'd take them to Hemet, and we would work and stay busy. Hemet was a trailer park that I had bought a few years earlier with Bones from his grandpa, and it was full of meth addicts. About forty families lived there. Things seemed to be going really well for a period, and then, just like that, we stopped getting referrals from other treatment centers because we had been blacklisted.

I didn't know why we were blacklisted by the others in the industry, because I knew that we were doing a really good job. I later found out why. All of those high-dollar treatment centers were designed for people to repeat. With us, we were actually healing people, getting them well, and denying others and ourselves all of the lucrative cash from having repeat clients. It was cynical and sad, but that was the way that the treatment centers worked back then. They saw people's addiction as being a cash cow. SOBA was different.

I saw a prospectus that was shown to me by a friend who wanted to team up with me. Treatment cost $60K, but they were averaging $180K per client, because most clients would come back three times. At that time, there were no treatment centers accepting insurance, so it was all cash out of pocket. It was a big-money industry.

Because treatment cost so much money, and because insurance companies weren't covering it back then, you mostly had superrich people in Malibu going to treatment centers. Every once in a while, you would run into a schoolteacher's kid, whose parents would have mortgaged their house, thinking they were sending them to the best centers. They could usually only afford thirty days—which didn't work. At SOBA, we started getting all of those kids. We would scholarship most of the kids. We would have $100K in income, and $300K in scholarships. We barely made it. There were so many times during those early days when our doors were threatened to be shut because of finances, but I just kept pushing along. I kept the faith. I knew that SOBA existed for a reason. I kept telling people that the only reason we were successful was because we kept showing up. We showed up one more day than all of the others who had quit.

Back in those days, everyone said that you couldn't treat a husband and a wife. It simply wouldn't work. So, I leased a condo up the street so that their whole family could stay there. The entire treatment community made a big fuss about me breaking rules that didn't actually exist. I did it, and that family was successful. They've been clean eight years. One of them actually works for me at one of my treatment centers. Word began to spread about SOBA, about our success, about our willingness to do anything and everything to help others. We started getting more and more clients coming to us, so we decided to expand. We started a detox.

Our expansion led us to the next step: we applied for a license. One day an inspector showed up at the facility because there had been a complaint by a disgruntled employee. She showed up and saw how nice things were. I told her that we weren't going to be able to survive, and that we had been waiting for our license. She called the state on our behalf and was told that the state inspections were on hold due to budget reasons. She was also told that the budget concerns had been alleviated and that things were back on, and that the man had just pulled my application. He told her that he had a stack on applications on his desk that were literally two feet high, and since someone was late to a meeting, he reached into the pile and pulled out an application. That random application that he pulled out, happened to be SOBA's. God had shown up in my life once again. The inspector came down, inspected, and approved my license.

Our expansion continued, and we started outpatient treatment. We also learned that none of the other treatment centers accepted insurance at this time. Your treatment center had to be JCAHO approved. JCAHO stood for Joint Commission on the Accreditation of Health Care Organizations. It was a stringent inspection. In order to obtain JCAHO certification, we were audited on medical, psychiatric, therapeutic, spiritual, nutrition, fitness, and social dimensions. I filled out the request for accreditation.

We did everything that we could to spruce the place up in order to meet all of the certification requirements. I took my storage shed, put in bamboo floors and walls, some mood lighting and candles, and called it a Chi room. I used the exercise equipment from the ranch to create a gym. It turned out that all of my efforts came together; we were the first accredited center in Malibu.

After our accreditation, we started getting respect from the other centers in Malibu. But we were still struggling. We could now accept insurance, but the insurance companies didn't want to give much money to help people. They would go through the bill, line by line, and eliminate everything. They denied services if you forgot to dot an *i*, or cross a *t*. So, we had to learn how to do our own billing. We did, and we started SOBA billing. So now, we had the residential treatment center, we had SOBA billing, SOBA living, and SOBA outpatient. Still, at the time, there was never any money, and we would have to offset. We would still need to have some people paying money so we could still treat the insurance clients.

Dr. Sharma showed up, and by this time, I was tired and worn out. I had the treatment center, two SOBA living complexes, one in Malibu, and one in Santa Monica, and two outpatient centers. He offered to buy SOBA from me, and I thought that I was ready to give it up. I got to the point of agreeing and reading the contract. From reading the contract, it seemed as though it would only benefit me. Everything seemed like a done deal . . . until he insulted me. His insult was the spark that I needed. It kind of renewed my vigor. I asked Dr. Sharma to go away and not come back, and I shredded the contracts on the spot.

Two days later, I was giving my next-door neighbor, Ronnie, a ride to the hardware store, and I mentioned that it was sad that I couldn't treat people with insurance unless I had cash clients. I needed someone to factor in my receivables. Little did I know that he would go to my neighbor on the other side, Shelia Becker, and tell her, and that they would come back with a million dollars for me to help people. After that, everything changed. SOBA was here to stay.

On the personal front, my sobriety continued. I would soon be coming up on my 4th sober birthday/anniversary, which was December 15th. Andrea's birthday was Dec 10th, so we decided to take a Disney Cruise to celebrate both events.

We were going on the cruise with championship boxer Steven Luevano and his family, and it was the first time we had ever really planned a trip. Usually we do things at the last minute or spur of the moment. So we go to Orlando and we get on the ship, and the ship takes us to The Bahamas, where the first tour was the beach at the Atlantis Resort. We find out that Steven's family didn't buy the right tickets to get in to Atlantis, so I tell Andrea to go and get the money back for our tickets. At first they refuse, so I had her go back and try again. She goes back and gets the money back, and she and I take off on our own little separate adventure. We go walking on the beach next to the resort, where I decide to go body surfing. I go out into the water and I get caught by a giant wave, which throws me back onto the beach, where I land the wrong way. I could feel my neck break, and I actually heard the snap.

I am paralyzed on my right side, and I am desperately gripping the sand to keep myself from getting pulled back into the ocean by the current. I found that I couldn't speak or call out, not even to my son Vincent who is right in front of me. Steven sees me, and quickly realizes that something is wrong, so he runs over and pulls me out of the water.

I didn't want to go to the doctorin the Bahamas, because I feared that the treatment wouldn't be up to par, so I waited and went to the medical office back on the ship.

Back on the ship, the doctor was this guy from some Third World country and could barely speak English, and the medical equipment onboard the ship was antiquated to put it nicely. The doctor gave me some Tylenol and told me to go back to my room and rest. I literally had to hold my neck in place, and I could feel it swelling up more and more with each passing minute.

Later that evening, I asked the doctor if I could get a massage to alleviate the pain, and he clears me. I go to the massage therapist, and she leans into me like I'm a professional football player who just finished playing a big game. The pain was unbearable.

Our ship eventually arrives back in Orlando and we fly back to Malibu, but the pain is too much for me. The swelling around my neck makes me look like I'm wearing some type of African tribal necklace. Andrea sends me to her friend who is a chiropractor, and she immediately sends me to the emergency room clinic. Once at the clinic, I can tell that its bad.

The perform a CAT Scan, and the guy comes out while I'm standing on the corner outside, and tells me that I have a broken neck. He tells me to wait, and someone will call me. The next thing I know, I'm getting a call from a surgeon from Cedar Siani, who is leaving a Christmas party to rush to his office. He has me meet him at his office.

It turns out that the specialist is a neuro surgeon, and he tell me that my T1 is broken, and that C1 and C2 on my spine were compression fractures. The doctor was literally in shock, and he doesn't know what to do. He tells me that usually when he sees an injury like this, he is rushing the patient to surgery to see how they can save the patient's life, or keep him from becoming a paraplegic. He places me in a neck brace, tells me not to move my head, and tells me that he'll give me a call when he figures things out.

Apparently the doctor went back to his Christmas party afterward, and I was the subject of much conversation, because the next morning the doctor has a colleague who owns an MRI center come in and open it up just for me. When I arrive at the place, the doctor, along with another surgeon, have my X-ray photos lining the wall and examining them. This second surgeon, and been called back from his Christmas vacation. He tells me that he has never seen these types of injuries on a human being that was still alive. He is amazed.

The doctors show me on film that a bone fragment has lodged into my spinal cord. They concur that is is a miracle that I am still alive, let alone walking. I walked out of that clinic thinking about my life, about SOBA, about God, and about my mission. I was in tremendous pain, but the last thing that I wanted to do, was start taking pain killers.

About a month later, my friend Ken asked me if I ever asked God, why me? I thought about his question briefly, and I explained the extent of my injuries to Ken, and then informed him that I do in fact ask God that very question. Not why it was done to me, by why He spared me and allowed me to not only live through it, but come out walking.

I stayed in my neck brace for about five months, and on the sixth month, I got a call from the surgeon telling me that I was still on his mind, and that he had been worried about me. He knew that I had lousy insurance, and he knew that I had jettisoned my neck brace, so he offered to help me out. He would do the surgery to repair my neck and spine, if I could come up with ten grand. I came up with the money, and six months after my accident, I underwent surgery and came out of it with a plate and some screws in my neck and spine.

On the business front, the first years of SOBA were still touch and go, even with the substantial loan from my wonderful neighbors. There were stretches when we didn't know if we were going to make it from month to month. It wasn't until Justin Pits and Alex Field learned how to do billing that things really turned around for us. The two of them got into the books and learned all of the things that we could actually bill for, and we started billing correctly and gaining resources. I remember walking into the office one day and seeing the board that they used to track resources coming in, and asking them if that was the money we had coming in. When they answered yes, I felt an enormous sigh of relief. I knew that we would be able to help a lot of people.

At that time, other treatment centers were just like us, in that they didn't know how to do billing. I got an idea, and figured that my proposal would be a winning situation for everyone; I started doing their billing for them. In addition to doing their billing for them, I became partners with these companies, and helped them set up long term treatment and business plans for success. SOBA quickly went from having six beds, to hundreds of them. We spread from Malibu, over the mountains, and into the valley. So did our reputation, our success, and our clientele.

As success begin to set in, our mission and our commitment to others never changed. We were never in it for the money, we had always been in it to help others, and that remains true to this day. I remember when we were getting JCAHO certified, I asked the guy doing the certification what was the biggest factor in successful treatment was, and he told me that it was length of time in recovery, staying connected to your treatment, and therapy, and treatment environment. So we set out to provide that.

Everything that we did at SOBA was designed to fill in the gaps that were missing. We had the initial residential treatment, and so we plugged in the outpatient, and the sober living facilities as well. Back then in Malibu if you didn't have fifty thousand in cash, you weren't walking into a treatment center. And even if you did have the cash, those centers were set up for you to fail. They wanted you to come back multiple times. SOBA was designed for the guys who didn't have fifty thousand dollars to spend getting well. We were the first to accept insurance, the first to do outpatient, and the first to establish a long term treatment option. The centers who did start to accept insurance, were state funded, and the quality of care was not there. In contrast, at SOBA, we offered a holistic, spiritual, and psychological approach to recovery. We can get anyone off of drugs relatively quickly, but mending a person's spirit and giving them back their value as human beings, takes time. That is what we focused on, and that's what made us such a success. It's also what has allowed us to take our healing across the country.

SOBA's expansion across the nation was almost happenstance. I remember being at the dentist when I got a call from my old friend Alex, who wanted me to put him in contact with Daniel Baldwin. Alex was doing a movie in San Antonio called HOA, and he wanted Daniel to come on board. Alex and I had started a small film company called Malibu Films near the beginning of my recovery, and hadn't done anything with it. I saw it as a wonderful opportunity to get Malibu Films going. We immediately revamped Malibu Films, and got to work on a second film called Wisdom, that was about recovery.

We were all in San Antonio on doing a morning show to promote the film, when Daniel starts promoting SOBA, and says on live television that we're going to donate the proceeds to a recovery center in San Antonio. Being that it had been said on live television, I had been cornered. I sent Alex a list of centers in San Antonio to donate the money to, and we found out that they were all methadone clinics. It was then when I learned that San Antonio, Central Texas, and the entire Rio Grande Valley was lacking a real, residential treatment center that utilizes a holistic approach to recovery. I immediately asked Alex to start looking for a place for SOBA to expand so that we could help people in Texas. He found a beautiful ranch nestled in the hill country on the outskirt of town. SOBA Texas quickly became a reality.

After the film Wisdom started getting recognition and winning awards, we hit the film circuit to promote it. It was during that tour when I heard Daniel talk about how much the film Wisdom meant to him, and so many others. He said that if it hadn't been for Wisdom, he wouldn't have been in San Antonio, and he wouldn't have promised that money, and we wouldn't have realized the dearth of effective treatment centers in the area, and so SOBA Texas wouldn't have been born. He credits the film Wisdom to saving all of the lives that have passed through SOBA Texas and gotten better.

After SOBA Texas, my eyes turned back West. We had been receiving a lot of clients in Malibu that hailed from the Phoenix area. Unfortunately, a lot of these clients had legal issues that they needed to take care of, while in the process of getting their lives back on the right track. We would send clients back to Phoenix, and that would get locked up, and we would lose them. Losing clients is something that we take personal, and we feel each lose deeply. We decided to do something about it. We opened a SOBA treatment facility in Mesa, Arizona.

About the time that SOBA Mesa opened, I had a former client finally put together his proposal to open up a SOBA treatment facility in New Jersey. He had always been passionate about opening up a treatment center geared toward college students. We are all familiar with the amount of drinking and drug abuse that occurs on college campuses across the nation. SOBA had been going into colleges and treating students from the beginning, but finally, a real partnership opportunity emerged.

Rutgers University is a real progressive university that understands treatment and recovery, and instead of sweeping things under the rug like the vast majority of universities and colleges across the country, they chose to step forward and allow us to treat with them. And so SOBA New Jersey became a reality, and is at the forefront of treating college kids on the East coast. We have gone from six beds in a tiny renovated motel structure, to more than five hundred beds across the country. We are at the forefront of recovery, putting families back together again, and healing a new generation facing the horrors of addiction on campuses across the country. Founding and running SOBA is not the life that I thought I would have, but I wouldn't change it for anything in the world. I get to spend my life helping others.

I think back on my life, on everything that I've been through, my addictions, the loss of several children, the number of times I've been in imminent danger, and I marvel at the miracle that has been my life. I left home at an early age, traveled and lived on the streets, going door-to-door selling newspapers and magazines so that I could have the next meal. I think about the beatings that I received because I refused to be a monster and beat someone else. I think about the loss of life on the road, the disappearances, the drowning, the runaways who were just trying to survive. I can still see them. I can see their faces, their smiles, the small victories that came with the sale of something so simple as a magazine subscription. I think about that industry, about changing it, about making it safer. I knew that something was wrong. No kids should have to die just because they wanted to sell a magazine in order to buy something to eat or have a safe motel room to lay their head for the night.

I think about my life in Seattle, the ocean, the cold, the rain, the beauty and majesty of the ocean from my dock on Fox Island. I think about the move to Vegas, the ranch, the animals, the shows, the boxing matches. And then I think about the drugs. The emptiness in my soul, the darkness in the desert and in the recesses of my mind, the howling of the animals in the desert and my begging for them to end my pain. I think about all of the times I pulled my father's gun out, just wanting to end the pain. I think about my battles with God.

I remember being left on that air force base in Louisiana, and I remember spending the rest of my life trying to not get left behind. I spent my life making noise, living on the edge, running and trying to catch up to something, without knowing what that something was. I lived my life with a fear that I was forgetting something, with a fear of being forgotten. So many times I was terrified that God had forgotten about me. Each time I shot up meth, or heroin, or smoked pot or crack, I felt as if God had forgotten about me. Each time I rushed Andrea to the hospital, and each time we lost a baby, I felt as if God had forgotten about me. I spent my life being one of the forgotten ones.

At least that's what I thought.

Each time it was time for me to move forward; God made a way forward. Each step that I took in the direction of Malibu, God made a way. I later came to realize that God had not forgotten about me or forsaken me, but had simply cleared a path for me in another direction. My calling wasn't in Las Vegas; it was in Malibu. My calling wasn't in playing tennis; it was in healing. I'm not a boxing promoter, a car salesman, an urban clothing owner, nor a rap label owner. My destiny wasn't to go to Arizona State, but to hit the streets of America, to go door-to-door, to live on the streets and in seedy motels. Why? So that I could look mothers and fathers and loved ones in the face and tell them that I understand what their child and loved ones are going through.

God took me to, and brought me through, the unspeakable nightmare of addiction so that I could bring others out of that nightmare. All my life I thought that I was running to catch up and not be left behind, when really, I was running toward the destiny that God had in store for me. The emptiness that I felt in my soul while dwelling in my desert of loneliness has been filled a thousand times over. Each letter, phone call, e-mail, text, and hug that I have received, thanking me for saving the life of a loved one, of a child, or from my clients themselves, bring a joy and fulfillment to my life that is inexplicable. God led me to SOBA to restore families, to save our young, and to use my life as a living, breathing testament to the power of His Grace, His Mercy, and His Redemption.

God is good, God is alive, and trust me, God has a plan for each and every one of us, even though we don't understand it and cannot see it. Never give up hope and always keep the faith.

And Jesus said unto them: "For truly, I say to you, if you have faith like a grain of mustard seed, you will say to this mountain, 'Move from here to there,' and it will move, and nothing will be impossible for you."—Matthew 17:20

L to R: Hannah Hannley, Greg Hannley,
Andy Dick, Meg Dick, Scotty Brown

Will Ferell & Greg Hannley

Greg Hannley & Ben Stiller

Greg Hannley & Andy Dick

Greg Hannley & U.S. Senator Corey Booker

Greg Hannley & Congressman Donald Norcross

Greg Hannley & Bill Zane

Greg Hannnley, Dr. Phil, Daniel Baldwin, Alex Draghici

Made in the USA
Lexington, KY
26 November 2016